Joy (handwritten)

THE GIFT OF POWER

by
Earnest Larsen, C.SS.R.

PAULIST PRESS
New York / Paramus / Toronto

Library of Congress
Catalog Card Number: 74-76715

ISBN: 0-8091-1833-5

Published by Paulist Press
Editorial Office: 1865 Broadway, N.Y., N.Y. 10023
Business Office: 400 Sette Drive, Paramus, N.J. 07652

Printed and bound in the
United States of America

CONTENTS

PART I
THE GIFT OF POWER

1. VISION

We are a very power-conscious people. We love power. All kinds of it. Power to make the car windows go up and down, power to run our sparkling new machines that cut our grass and wash our dishes. We literally spend millions of dollars a year to acquire the skill which gives us the power to make people like us, to become physically beautiful, slim or strong. We, perhaps, prize nothing so much as power.

A noted psychiatrist defines power as "the ability to effect or prohibit change." That is what we love —to be in control of change. At times, in our secret heart, we come close to coveting witchcraft. How wonderful it would be to have magical power: at the wave of a wand or wrinkle of a nose we could make all sorts of wondrous things happen. With this kind of power at our command we could not only take care of our personal needs and whims, but end poverty, wipe out war, destroy all the kitchens of crime. It's all a matter of power.

It is. Yet anyone who comes among us proclaiming, "REJOICE! THE LORD HAS RISEN! WE HAVE ACCESS TO THE POWER OF GOD," is considered either a religious fanatic or suitable material for a mental ward. And yet it is true. The meaning of Christ is the meaning of power. Unending, limitless, unstoppable power. We have but to understand the nature of this gift God offers us in Christ and claim it. Claim it so that it is ours.

Let us ponder this most thrilling of all human phenomena: the gift of power. Not just force, but authentic power. The ability to change not just things but people. Change as the closed bud of a rose is changed when it is bathed in the warming rays of the sun; changed in the dimension of being opened, set free, so that the scent of the rose is able to be carried on the wind to all who would avail themselves of its loveliness. Even to the most tightly closed, the most terrified and wounded, the scent of the freed rose stands without and knocks. Who knows? Perchance through some unguarded crack the rose will enter and slowly, infallibly touch that which was dead bringing it to life, soften that which was atrophied. And suddenly, where before there was a withered, locked flower, now there is a new witness to the power of sun and wind—another blooming rose lifting its head to the light and casting its scent upon every breeze that passes by.

 The power enabling us to become free so that we may in turn share in the healing of one another is a gift. It begins outside ourselves and slowly, or like a thunderous storm, invades our consciousness. Like the tightly locked flower, try as we may we cannot say the rose is not there when it stands at our very center. Like the closed flower, we must either die all together or become one with the Lover who stands within, inviting us to bloom.

The gift of power is the gift of love. People are not flowers. Flowers can bloom without love (although many studies, strangely enough, indicate that if even flowers are loved they bloom to a new and greater beauty). People cannot bloom without love. All human beings need to know in the only way that counts, by it happening, deep in their consciousness that they are loved and, therefore, lovable. Yet, like flowers planted in dark, obscure places, how many humans there are who neither know nor expect ever to discover that they are precious beyond words. The gift of power has never flooded their consciousness. The option to bloom has never occurred to them. The gentle breeze carrying the scent of life has never caressed their souls.

But it can; that is the point. That is the wondrous, delirious, magnificent point: IT CAN HAPPEN. Jesus has given us that gift in His resurrection. If only we would but truly believe and claim the power given us by Our Lord. If only we would lift our heads and hearts to the wind and allow the irresistible fragrance of a free human being, who acknowledges that he has been named and claimed by God Himself, to be carried to the world. If only we would accept the gift of Power.

In such frightful desperation our hearts strain to have some realistic hope of lifting our heads up and shouting in joy: BLESSED BE GOD! THE WORLD IS NOT DOOMED! WE ARE NOT A DYING RACE!

We look up from fantastically overcrowded colleges and schools, from work schedules that are neither creative nor satisfying, from an inner gloom fed by disillusionment in leadership and deep spiritual hunger and say, is there hope? Is there REALLY any reason to keep on struggling? Is there any power that can save us? Any magic that will keep the lions at bay as Daniel was saved in the desperate pit in which he found himself?

Yes, yes, I know Christ died and rose. I'm not asking that. I'm asking if there is any power that can save us.

Perhaps we do not always accept what we know. Maybe there is a chasm between knowing and believing. It could be that we are not too unlike skeptics who stood around a tomb thousands of years ago. What was natural and expected had happened—death. There was one, a man named Christ, who claimed the absurd power of mastery over death. The skeptics, of course, denied it. What a shock they had in store for them as they stood around in their ritual pose of mournful wailing on that fateful day.

Lazarus had died. His sisters had buried him last week. Life simply was no more. The rose had fallen from the stem. Rumor had it that the sisters of Lazarus had called upon a prophet named Jesus, a dear friend of theirs, to come to them in their hour of need. That was days ago. He had not shown up. Yet, on the fourth day after burial, here He came walking down the road with His followers. He was indeed a strange one, this man Christ. He claimed such unheard-of power, spoke of such marvelous, if unrealistic, visions of what could be. No, not only of what could be, but of what is. He defined reality.

But no matter; Lazarus is dead and that is that.

Foolishly the sisters of the dead man ran to Christ. They are out of their minds. Do you hear what they are saying:

Dead? I thought you knew better than that. Don't you believe—I am the Resurrection and the Life.

"Oh, Jesus, we know that. At the end of time you will come and raise all of us who have died. In that far away day you will have power. That isn't what we are concerned with. Our brother is dead now, in this life. That is what gives us such sorrow."

But I keep telling you, I am master of THIS LIFE! Somehow that doesn't break through very well. This world, this earth, and all that moves in it is my concern, that is where I take my stand. I am concerned with life and death right here and now. Why can't you hear that? If only you would believe, you would have life in abundance.

Even the sisters, who loved Jesus, didn't hear His word. But they began to wonder. A strange light started to dawn in their faces. This Christ was a strange, powerful man. Do you suppose, do you RE-ALLY suppose He is going to do something about our brother's passing away? Their thoughts painted the sky of their souls with brilliant hope.

Call him out of death, Lord. Tell him to put away the things of the grave. Make it possible for him to take off the rotten, stinking rags of death and march out from the cave tomb. Walk out into the light. You speak so often of life. But Lazarus is dead. Make life possible in the midst of death. Call him.

The voice of the Carpenter rolled out on that cloudy day like a clap of thunder over pounding waves.

LAZARUS—Come Forth!

Stupid. The man is dead. Is this silly prophet crazy? What is He talking about? "Come Forth!" Who does He think He is? Does He suppose to have power over death itself?

So many of the mourners, those who never

thought things could ever change, laughed Him to scorn.

LAZARUS—Come Forth!

Some others held their breath. There was a feeling of power in the air. The dry, electric feeling that some huge event was about to take place. Some wept as if they knew what was about to come. Some mocked. Man just doesn't have the option of life over death. When you are dead, you are just dead.

LAZARUS—Come Forth!

Groaning was heard. A shadow inched its way out of the tomb. There, from the gloom of that cave of death, stumbled a dead-man-returned. Horrendous shock waves must have gripped all those whose eyes were riveted on the mouth of the grave giving back one it had taken. The winding sheets were still clinging to flesh that should have been deep into the process of decay. What was under the napkin covering the head? Were the sockets of the eyes filled again with organs of sight? Could his hands feel the good things of the earth? Would his tongue be able to sing, to talk to his friends? Was he really alive?

Jesus, the giver of the gift of life, calmly told the beloved of Lazarus to take off the strips of cloth which held their brother and give him something to eat. He had come back whole and entire.

What a thrill it would have been to see that dead man walk out of the tomb. In the presence of one come back to life there is scant room for skeptics. Yet we have seen, daily if we but take the time to look, flowers of the rarest beauty blooming where once there stood but sterile sticks. Skeptics are nothing new; it is just that in a world filled with the brothers of Lazarus, they don't make much sense.

Jesus does have a gift to give. His power was and is the very power of life over death, of calling that which was dead to walk forth again into life. Jesus does offer Lazarus and us that option. He could bring life from death because He was willing to get down on the razor's edge of death itself. You can only give one to the extent you are willing to suffer the other. Gifts are like that.

You really don't see as much genuine gift-giving happening these days as you would like. That's a tragedy. Many people say the world is growing dark and ugly. Maybe it is exactly because we have forgotten what it means to give and receive gifts.

It isn't that a lot of things aren't being exchanged; they are.

China has given the United States two panda bears and we have given them musk oxen. Lots of people give money gifts to the cancer or heart foundations.

Aunt Beulah gives all the kids presents at Christmas; there are anniversary gifts, graduation gifts, ordination gifts, wedding gifts. In fact, it gets to be a major problem of what to give at those designated gift-giving times of year.

But that is the whole point—when a gift becomes a problem, it no longer is a gift. When the only season of giving is at "designated times," the season never really comes. Gifts are not things. The fantastic life-giving power of gifts is that they are merely a way in which one person gives himself to another. Any gift that is not but an instrument upon and through which we play the song of who we are, is just a thing in nice wrapping. It might be expensive or even needed. But it is not a gift.

That is hard to get hold of. For some reason many people can't understand why a child lovingly hangs onto a ten-cent gift and is willing to give away a ten-dollar thing. But the gift was given by someone the child knew loved him. It was more than just the thing; it was an instrument singing the sweetest of songs.

Or you hear quite often legally married people confused about, "What more do they want? I give them all they ask for! They had a roof over their heads, clothes on their backs, food on the table. What do they want? Christmas cost me $500 last year." Mighty expensive.

Lots of things were given, but no gifts. Take back the mink coat, give me a hug; I don't want the new encyclopedia; what I want is the knowledge that you care what happens to me; the car is really nice, but it is not half as nice as knowing you care enough about me to get it.

Then we stand around in wide-eyed bewilderment saying, "I don't get it. What is the problem?" Gifts and giving are hard things to get hold of.

The amazing thing about gifts is what power they have. Not being mainly things but people in the form of things they have the power of creation itself. On the cloudiest day, a real gift can call the sun into being. On the coldest day, one who has received a genuine gift feels warm, safe and protected. No matter how desperate the hour or how fierce the battle, the giving of a gift beats back the wolves and calls a halt to war.

"Hi" can be a gift money can't buy. "You don't look so well to me; is anything wrong?" can be a medicine that will never be put in a pill or bottle.

"You are as welcome as the flowers in spring" can be an authentic calling to life out of the tomb of death. It is a shame there isn't more gift-giving going on. We are all wasted without it.

Alice is only five, but she knows all about the need for and the giving of gifts. She is deaf and lives in a school-home especially for the deaf. A young man named Mike visits there from time to time. He is a Christ-man giving the very gift of Jesus himself: life.

Whenever Mike comes, he could bring Alice a toy, flowers, games. He doesn't. The gift he does bring is himself. Each time Alice sees him she runs wildly into his arms and Mike invariably touches her nose.

The roof of the Sistine Chapel in Rome is decorated with a scene of this encounter. Michelangelo must have known all about Mike and Alice in 1513 when the work of art was painted. There he has the hand of God reaching out to the grasping hand of man. They almost touch—one waiting for the gift to be given, one about ready to give. There is the same expectancy of powerful electricity in the scene, of the flow of getting-up-life that one can feel in the words of Christ commanding Lazarus to come forth, and can be seen in the face of Alice receiving her gift from Mike, and Mike rejoicing in the fruit of the gift being given. Which itself is a gift.

Gifts are like that; they are not things but people singing their song through material objects. Through a touch, a kiss, a song. Jesus was continually in the process of giving his gift, of offering the option of life over death.

Mary—Come Forth!

Mary? She is the village whore. What is He talking about this time? She is what she is. Nobody can change that. Some people are just born to lose; she is one of them. Christ should be a realist. The option for that fallen woman to change just isn't to be had.

Mary—Walk away from that tomb you are living in!

Wow! He makes me nervous messing with that woman. I wish He would leave her alone. He keeps talking of a vision of something better. Like what? He keeps sticking up for her as if she really isn't a bad person. Let her be! If she didn't like what she was doing, she wouldn't do it. It looks so bad for Him, a holy man, to be talking to her. What will people think?

Granite-faced, eyes burning like pools of liquid steel, Christ stood before that tomb. He walked through the very gates of hell with His gift just as He would commission His apostles under Peter to do another day.

Mary—Come out of there.

Oh, but we caught this woman in adultery . . . Mary, I am calling you! . . . She is nothing but a slut, a dog. . . Mary, it is I, do not be afraid! . . . Why does she waste that precious ointment on Christ; we could have put it to better use . . . Mary, I am calling you out of death.

As surely as dead Lazarus got up from the world of the dead, this woman stepped forth from her grave. She put aside the clothing of the deceased and decorated her soul with the flowers of the living. She learned the meaning of belief in what is good, learned to touch and feel again, what it meant to suffer for that which you love, to eat the bread of genuine affection. She was willing to pay the price to be alive, which is to pay the price of growing.

As a result of the Christ-gift, her eyes saw strange, new wonders. They were at hand all the time but her death kept her from seeing them. She was able to see little deaf Alice, who was living in her time as well; she was able to extend the same gift to the same spirit of this little girl through the gentle touching of a small nose.

Her eyes began to see what was good in people, to expect the best and not the worst from them. Cynicism drained out of her like infection from a lanced wound. To expect nothing but death from others is to encourage it. Mary became a different woman.

There came the day when they took the Gift-giver to a hill and murdered Him. It was no place for the faint of heart to gather. All those who would declare themselves for Christ on that day would stand alone. But the gift had made her new. On the Hill of Skulls was "Mary His mother . . . and Mary from whom He had driven seven devils." Devils of death.

The "realistic" vocal people who laughed when Christ stood before Mary's tomb calling her to step forth were not there. They had not as yet received the gift of Christ. They were operating on their own power, marching to their own thin tunes of popularity and fear. They were hiding. It was the woman who had come back from the dead who was where they should have been.

Mary of Magdalen lives in our world just as deaf little Alice lived in hers. The gift of Christ aches to leap forth from the hand of God now just as it did then. The same death pervades our world as in all ages past, and the same options are open to us now as were to Lazarus and Mary in the hour of their days on earth. Things really haven't changed much.

And because they haven't changed, because that option for life is with us, we are free to shout RE-JOICE! AGAIN I SAY REJOICE! For Christ has won the victory. That victory is His gift to us. He has taken all the misery and failure of His people and dealt with it. God made it His business in Christ. Death has been defeated. The option of every individual to overcome the death in his life and mankind as a whole to grow into a human family, is possible. The gift has been given to us that we may extend it to others.

2. CONSCIOUSNESS

The gift of Jesus was a gift of increased consciousness, a gift of power and life. Where before there was darkness, He cast light; where before there was no choice but to perish in the blind worship of false gods, Christ offered an option through His gift of another way to go. Lazarus had no option but to be dead until Christ came and called him forth. Mary would be no more than she was until the Carpenter passed into her life like a raging storm of goodness, and through the gift of His spirit, offered her something better.

Consciousness is like that. It always offers a choice. Where before there was something I did not know or was not aware of—now, through the gift of a Giver, I become aware of something new. This discovery of truth gives me a new direction to go, contingent upon the fact that I make a decision to choose the way. Our concrete world takes its shape and its form from the decisions made at that crossroads.

This process of revealing of truth, to option being available, to decision being made, to those decisions forming our concrete existence, is present on every level of our lives and world. It is true in business matters: if I knew a new superhighway was going through this part of town, I might or might not choose to buy appropriate land and thereby risk

making a lot of money. If I didn't know of the highway construction, I would do nothing.

It happens in a thousand simple little ways in
which we run our lives: if I knew it was going to
rain, I might or might not take an umbrella with me;
if I knew the school bus had a flat tire, I might or
might not choose to get to the pick-up point on time;
if I had known an old acquaintance from the army
was going to be in town, I might or might not have
made some decisions about being with him. (All options made possible through increased awareness.
Each option leading to a decision. Each decision
having a bearing on the concrete world in which I
live.)

But there are many deeper levels than these on
which the same process is taking place. These levels
have to do with an understanding of the persons we
are, and who those people are with whom we dwell
on this planet. I would not shoot my brother, yet
thousands of people are shot every day. Are we not
all brothers separated but by the lack of awareness,
the understanding that this is so? Is the problem not
one of realization, of consciousness and apparent inability to make creative decisions based on that
knowledge?

This is precisely the point—Jesus came as des-
troyer of separating walls. He came as bridge over
separated islands, as light slamming its brightness
into every dark corner of humanity. There is no man
who cannot know that he is son of God, set free by
the free gift of Christ. There is no one who should
not know by the example and support of a Christian
community that he belongs. Those options are possible. Every man can know that the Lord Has Risen,

every man and the world as one CAN come from the tomb Lazarus-born. It is all possible, for the option has been given us. The truth has been revealed. Faith is a gift—but the gift has been given. As with all gifts, it but waits to be accepted. Such as with Joyce.

It was spring's most glorious day of the year. Outside the alcoholic rehabilitation center, the sun blazed as warm as a friendly handshake. The sky was blue and the wind made you simply happy to be alive. It was one of those days especially welcome after a long siege of cold and snow that automatically made people smile when passing one another. Even the meanest man was tempted to bend down and pat a dog's head and be thankful that the grass would soon be green.

Inside a group session was in process. Six residents of the center were discussing their fears, searching for light within the support and comfort of the others.

Walter didn't appear to be a particularly happy man. It was his third time through treatment, this being the second week of this third attempt at building a liveable life. His family had just been evicted from their home. Who would move them? Whose truck would haul the larger pieces of furniture? How would they manage with him in there?

Johnny sat next to him. He was a very tall man, nearly bald with a large black beard. He was a quiet man. He didn't think he had a problem, there really wasn't any reason for him to be there, even though he had just been through his second automobile crash which had totally demolished the car. Both times he was intoxicated.

Art was an Indian. At one time he had studied

for the ministry and was very well grounded in theology. Nearly everyone in the center leaned on Art. He was a very gentle man and the leader of this particular group.

Roy looked as if he were chiseled from black marble. He almost never spoke and his shaved head always seemed to be reflecting light from somewhere. He constantly wore a dark pair of sunglasses which properly fit as they should above his wiry beard. No one knew much about Roy—he said so little. No one knew his story. But it was agreed by all that although Roy seemed to possess immense strength, he had never hurt or threatened anyone at the center. As with many large men, he seemed to genuinely be a man of tenderness.

Brenda was back again as well. If ever a beautiful woman graced the stage of the world it was she. Only now, in her twentieth year, the definite lines of hardness and bitterness were etching themselves in her lovely face. The room had heard stories like hers for as long as the rehabilitation center had been operating. Born to a family where children were mistakes and love a nonexistent reality that often was laughed about. Laughed about even while its absence was the source of devastating starvation.

Brenda was on the street at 14. By the time she reached her sixteenth year, nothing of pain and hurt on this earth was a stranger to her. But she was different. There was some hunger or inner strength in her that wouldn't quite let her die. Even though she had never known the "good life" she wasn't quite willing to admit that it was not possible. She was reaching for it with every fiber of her heart. Alcohol and drugs had become a regular part of her existence. Yet always, at least so far, after a time she got herself admitted again to the center. To dry out and try again. Maybe "this" would be her time. Maybe this time around she would see something she had never seen before and be able to hang her life on it. So desperately she wanted the dream to translate into reality.

The last member of the session was Joyce. If body language speaks, she was screaming out with all her might, "I have been wounded. Please don't step on me further." Joyce had suffered a stroke sometime earlier that had left her right arm slightly paralyzed, her hand deformed. She had lived perhaps sixty years, most of them in hospitals or treatment centers of one kind or another, she had said. Even though her face was transparently white, it seemed there was a great darkness around her eyes. She was so thin it seemed she would simply cease to move at any given moment. But now, on this gorgeous, warm day she was speaking freely:

"Frances, it's Frances that gives me so much trouble. If only I could get away from her. For three years now she keeps telling me what a sinner I am. All she keeps talking about is that I am not strong enough to make it. She makes me feel so ugly." Everyone in the group was listening. Each and every one there had their own Frances.

Art spoke to her of being whole, of believing in herself.

Johnny said that none of them were as bad as everyone else said. After all, there was nothing wrong with him and he had still would up in this place.

Brenda didn't say much. She only spoke with

her eyes. They were filled with compassion and sympathy for this crushed, vulnerable lady who may well be a prediction of the future for herself.

"Like, why can't she let me be?" said Joyce. "I finally moved out from her house and got an apartment by myself. She kept telling me I couldn't make it without her. Then she got to be coming over and going through my mail and checking all the time if I had friends up or there was any drinking going on. It got so I had to drink just to keep my mind off her."

Walter's mind was a million miles away, as far away as his family. He was his own Frances. Day in and day out he scourged himself with the whip of guilt and self-hatred. If there ever was a loser in the world, in his mind it was he.

Joyce spoke on for another twenty minutes. "I'm so confused, always so confused about myself. I know I'm no good. I know all I have ever done is hurt people and mess up my life, but I don't want to be like this. But I always feel so rotten about myself."

It was one of the first times Roy had ever been heard to speak. His voice sounded almost like it came from outside the group, like it hadn't come from him at all. The room had been deathly silent and the huge black man's voice had rolled out like a drum, "Joyce, God made you and God don't make no junk."

It had sounded like thunder. In the quiet center of each one's soul, it had struck like lightning. Brenda, Johnny, Walter—God don't make no junk.

It was still a beautiful day hours after the session was over. Funny how most of the members of the group were not up in the dorms drowned in music or distracting themselves by reading or checkers. Nearly all of them were quietly walking around the grounds with a strange, lovely glow in their eyes.

Especially Joyce. She was sitting under a large tree, squarely in the middle of a shaft of golden sunlight. She didn't look very old or broken sitting there. By the shine in her eyes it appeared as if she might have caught hold of a most precious secret she had never heard before. A secret that could be the start of healing power.

Like streams leading to a river and rivers to the sea, this process can be seen at every turn of life. No one had the possibility of flying from San Francisco to New York until the puny, but indispensable illumination given us by the Wright brothers. Their discovery, their rendering of increased human consciousness, led man eventually to this possibility. Anyone is certainly free to make the trip or not, but the option is there.

The possibility of blood transfusions and delicate surgery has come to us by inching back the veil of darkness. Countless men, many of whom are totally forgotten, dueled ignorance and pushed back the frontiers of human awareness, thus leading to a decision to pursue the battle or let it lay. But upon this decision, our concrete world rests.

Every category of every phase of our lives exists within the context of this process. Awareness leading to truth. Truth leading to the option to choose, and choice leading to the molding of the quality of the world in which we exist.

Dr. Rollo May, a noted psychiatrist, speaks of an Italian artist named Giotto, who, for the first time in the early 14th century, decided that all art did not need to be two-dimensional. May points out that Giotto, who was the precursor of the Renaissance, saw nature in a new perspective for the first time. He painted rocks and trees in a three-dimensional space. It was not that this view had not been possible before, it was simply that no one had unveiled this possibility. Giotto, by his work, enlarged human consciousness because his perspective required an individual man standing at a certain point to see this perspective. The individual was now important, where up until this time it was eternity that was the sole criterion of how a man lived in this world. The art of Giotto was a prediction of the Renaissance individualism, which was to flower one hundred years later. As a result of this new view of space, this new unveiling of truth by the artist, the basic mental and spiritual insights were laid down whereby a Magellan and a Columbus could explore the ocean. It was the format upon which the explorations in astronomy by Galileo and Copernicus could take place. It was the forerunner of a revolutionary new way of man to see himself within the universe; and from this increased awareness, from this new view of the possibilities open to us, man has taken a step forward, never to be the same.

In much the same way, Kenneth Clark in his classic work *Civilization* explains how a monk, named Suger, in the late 11th and early 12th centuries by his view that we arise to the glory and beauty of God by contemplating and loving the beauty of this earth, laid down the foundation of mind and heart whereby the magnificent cathedrals of Europe were built. Up until this time, medieval man thought himself not as an individual, but as a part of the degenerate, sinful whole. Their concept was that since they were so sinful and God was so great they had no right to share in any beauty. They had no excuse to view themselves as lovable or worthy to build any lovely creation.

It was through this insight, the unveiling of this view of reality, that man was freed to build, not as an expression of pride but as a sign of acknowledging the glory of God, some of the greatest masterpieces of the Western world.

Suger, Giotto, the Wright brothers, and so many others have rendered the human community invaluable service by passing on to our hands the gift of consciousness whereby we lay hold of the power to make of our world what we will. Vision is the source of power. Yet all these men deal with particles of life. They are involved in their own arena of genius, their own theater of operation.

Jesus came not to illuminate one dimension of life, but to speak to man as he is. Man, in his total stance toward God, himself, the human community, and the world in which he takes his stand. Jesus came not merely to enlighten man with the power of knowledge that he could fly or paint three-dimensional art, but to confront man as a being standing before his Father. He speaks to man in the total context of his existence upon this planet.

As long as man has felt the civilizing urge to community, he has desperately struggled to free himself from the jungle within. As surely as the fiery sun has daily risen eons before the collective memory of mankind can recall, this fierce inner combat has raged in man's mind and heart. Amid all the agony borne of violence in our history, a softer, milder face, phantom-like, could be seen peering out in sorrow at the body-strewn field of Gettysburg, the massacre of Wounded Knee, the horror of almost forgotten names like Ypres, Verdun, Kaesong, and Hue. But there is another option.

This is the question of faith in the risen Christ. Jesus has given us the option. It does not have to be this way. Lazarus can march forth. The power necessary to rage against the encroachments of the inner jungle has been won. Christ has flooded into human consciousness the possibility of a better way; the realistic option, if man but so choose to make of himself and his world something better. It is possible if he allows the power of God to operate within him. For every Gettysburg, there is the power for a hand to be extended in the openness of reconciliation from brother to brother. For every Hue, there is the possibility of a Dr. Schweitzer or a Tom Dooley piping the tune of human creativeness, rather than destruction.

Can a believer help but proclaim in all honesty: REJOICE! THE VICTORY HAS BEEN WON! And this, not in spite of all the human misery around us, but in relation to it. What is more tragic for a starving man than to know there is no bread. Death for such a man is not a choice, but a certainty. Yet this same man has unbounded hope if he knows there is, indeed, nourishment to be had if he but reach out his hand. It is the difference between certain death and the choice for life.

Yes, this softer, kinder face of mankind is seen to weep before the sub-human living quarters created by the Industrial Revolution. It does, indeed, gag on the dense clouds of exploded gun powder, and the searing heat of napalm that seems to engulf our globe. It rebels at the death and coldness stalking unnumbered marriages, homes and relationships that should be creative wellsprings of life.

Like a sad-eyed child, the face to one who looks can be seen peeking out from behind the immense shields and sour masks hiding so many wounded brothers and sisters. In those rare moments when the masks flag, the face can be seen and heard to say, "Must it be like this?"

Rejoice! No, it doesn't, proclaims the believer. The Lord has given us an option. He has not only given us the vision that we are brothers gathered together under the same roof of humanity, but also under the Godship of one who is our Father, and He has given us the power to make this vision a reality. So many countless people ask sincerely, "Is love possible?" Rejoice! The answer is, "It certainly is!"

If any of us so choose to leave behind the anchors of pessimism to which we seem powerfully attached, we can fill our minds with fellow human beings who have not given up, who have not been broken. There are so many in both famous and unheralded instances who have stood against the insanity, pain-inflicting processes of our world. Like Don Quixote, they have charged the seemingly invincible windmill, and done battle with the "evil enchanter."

What the believer is called on to acknowledge, is that the windmill stands upon the Lord's field. It is within His hand and subject to His power working through His people. There, indeed, is the question: Who is mad? Who does "realistically" see life as it is? He who has a dream, or he who does not? When the fearsome comic warrior charged the windmill, could any believer help but almost weep? Weep with hope and joy at the power and the courage we have to conquer our hills.

Like children tiptoeing fearfully through a dark house at night, we seem at times to almost fear the very light we so loudly proclaim we need. Repeatedly, we encounter all the successful Don Quixotes, and then say, "Yes, but." But then the trumpet blasts. The enemy is in sight. Quicker than a witch casting a spell, the mellow face of humanity yearning for something better vanishes, to be replaced by the ageless curse of a cold granite stone face.

We say this as if proving that the coldness of human failure were the only option. All that it proves for the believer is that in each of these cases, the option to death took its toll, even while life was possible.

Christ came not to dance around the fringes of human life, but rather to take His stance within the very core of our power, to make His power *our* power. Our Lord was not merely being a master of rhetoric when He proclaimed, "I am the Light of the World. I am the Way and the Truth." It was, rather, a statement of God's intention to take man not as a hobby or an amusement, but to take him seriously in Christ. The meaning of Christ is the ability of man to both consciously combat his demons and win, as well as the power to never cease in our ability to grow as people capable of loving. The power is there. The option is available. The choice is ours.

3. DYING

Power is a gift. A gift dwelling within the consciousness of each man as he discovers his options to become more than what he is and to make the world more than what it is. It is the gift of the rose freely releasing its scent upon the wind for all to share in. It is a gift, however, not without its price tag. Jesus once told a parable about a grain of wheat.

Again, people are not flowers. A rose has no choice but to surrender its essence in fragrance upon the wind. People do have that choice. The clear-cut statement that "unless the grain of wheat falling into the ground dies, it remains alone; but if it dies, it bears fruit in abundance" leaves little room for interpretation. There is a mighty difference between withering away and dying in favor of a creative rebirth. If the wheat dies not, there is no bread.

All the rhetoric in the history of man never supplied one mouthful of bread for a hungry man. In just the same way, all the talk of the ages about gifts and power does not substitute for the process of dying that we may rise. The gift of Jesus is the gift of love, but there can be no loving without a dying.

Dying is not a once and for all action; it is a process. The result of this process is expressed in all that we do and say. It is the light in our eye that cannot be put there any other way. Father Kevin O'Shea quotes Laurens van der Post as saying, "The author was present at the liquidation of Dutch colonial rule in Indonesia. The departing Governor General turned to him and said: 'I cannot understand it. Look what we have done for them. Look at the hospitals and schools we have given them. We have done away with malaria, plague and dysentery. Everyone has enough to eat. We have given them an honest and efficient administration and abolished war and piracy. Look at the roads, the railways, the industries—and yet they want us to go. Can you tell me why they want us to go?' He replied: 'Yes, I think I can. I'm afraid it's because you never had the right look in your eye when you spoke to them.' It may sound inadequate but just think for one moment of the light that is in the eye of a human being when he looks at another human being he loves and respects as an equal." It is the light in your eye!

What light? What is he talking about? The light that comes with contending with our selfishness and ego that there might be room in our worlds for others. Everyone wishes the closed flowers of this world would suddenly become open. But it isn't sudden and doesn't happen accidently. The power of life derives its energy from the act of dying, from the wheat falling into the ground.

Andy had great hopes of one day becoming a rodeo champion. There is nothing he loved more than horses and riding. His father owned a ranch and to the boy of seventeen, it was the only place in the world. Then one night on a cold, rainy highway the dream ended in a car wreck.

Andy's right leg no longer can move by itself. It is like a lifeless extension dangling from his body. By pulling up from behind the knee he can put his leg in any position he chooses, but he cannot move it by himself. Nor can he get around without his pair of crutches. The doctors say there is no hope there will ever be improvement.

Andy's God moved out the second of the accident. The sweetness of life drained from his existence like air from a punctured tire. He desperately attempts not to be bitter and hostile toward his one-legged existence, but feels he is losing the battle. No one seems able to say much to Andy that makes any difference. That power just doesn't exist. If the bud of his life ever opens it will be a miracle. But sometimes miracles happen at parties.

Terry is Andy's loyal, beautiful friend. As often as the one-time rodeo hopeful tries to pull away from life, Terry is tugging the other way. So it happened that he managed to talk Andy into going to a party one night, crutches and all. Little did Lazarus know who would be there.

Sue is a lady who, as van der Post put it, has that light in her eye. Which seems a little strange, for she is blind. She lost one eye to cancer when she was three and the other one at age five. That was nearly twenty years ago. Since then she has graduated from college, gone on to get her Montessori teaching certificate, find an apartment of her own, master the guitar, banjo, autoharp, flute among other instruments, as well as sing like an opera star. In her college days she was a peace activist and marched with Martin Luther King, and gave strong witness to her desire that killing be outlawed. She tells anyone who cares to listen, "If you think I am a bit extraordinary, I'm not. It is simply the Lord working in me. It is His power, not mine."

Sue firmly believes a Christian should have something in his life, an outward sign, that marks him as different, set apart from non-Christians. A mark that denotes him not as superior, but symbolizes a willingness to be of service. For this reason she is a strict vegetarian.

It happened on this particular night that Sue stood without Andy's cave and beckoned him to come forth. And all evening long she didn't even know he was there. Andy, Terry and a few others were sitting on the floor on the other side of the room from Sue. The blind woman possessing such magnificent sight was busy about her constant involvement of celebrating life. She was too busy singing songs, meeting new people, finding out "what's new," fondling the soul of existence to be concerned about her own limitations. The grain of wheat was too busy bearing much fruit to even notice that it was dying.

Andy's eyes seldom left the singing woman. Like the skeptics of old who were silenced as the grave gave back one it had taken, he could do nothing but admit in the presence of life conquering death that it was possible. She had every bit as much right to drown in self-pity and bitterness as he. But she wasn't. She had as much reason to limit the expectations of what she could or couldn't accomplish as he had done. But what had she left undone that she might have been able to do with physical sight? She had every right to die, but chose life instead.

Wondrous things were happening behind the boy's eyes. The ripples of that mental stirring could be clearly seen in his face. He didn't have to die! There apparently was no reason why he had to wrap himself in the shroud of a grave and call that home.

Sue spoke no physical word to Andy the whole evening. Her spirit was the word being spoken, a word of life and power. A spirit made powerful through claiming the power of her Lord that she might die and in the process become the bread feeding a vast number.

Were she to speak to Andy they would understand the meaning of Calvary. Sue knew all about the temptation to cry out in anger, "Why me! What did I ever do to you, God, that you did this to me!" She knows all about the agony of having to endure painful remarks from insensitive people. She understands what it means to be left out of what other "normal" people are doing. So well she understands how these things can so easily become the center of life, leaving no room for anything else.

But it doesn't have to be that way. There is an option. The option of the Risen Lord to place the narrow boundaries of her life within the wider context of Himself. She had the option of letting go of the futile effort to run her own life and allow God to use her as His instrument to feed the hungry. She chose that option and in doing so, gave her life over to God as she understood Him. From that point on God's power was hers. No one had the power to reach Andy until he ran into Sue. He still might not choose the direction Sue has chosen, but he cannot deny the scent of the rose standing within the crumbled walls of his hopes and dreams.

There is a strange, common quality about all the Sues in the world, all of those possessed of the power gained from dying that they might live. Every one of them is a celebrator of life. Each and every

one of them is beauty-oriented. It most certainly is
not that they live in a fanciful world admitting of no
pain or ugliness. Quite the opposite. You usually
find that the genuine lovers of life are more involved
with the wounded than any others. It is that their
eyes work differently. From their perspective of the
Resurrection, what they see is different from what
their brothers, who have not made the passage, are
aware of.

Where one sees failure, the other sees a not yet
totally unsuccessful struggle to succeed; where one
sees ugliness, the other sees incomplete beauty;
where one is aware of darkness, the other is aware of
the approaching dawn; where one sees a criminal,
the other sees the natural result of painful, unful-
filled needs; where one sees hatred, the other sees
unclaimed love; where one sees the need for violence,
the other offers the power of the rose.

The consciousness of the gift-givers is different.
It is precisely that they see themselves not as givers
but as receivers. From their view of things they are
much less concerned with activity than with the
power of passivity. They know that it is in letting go
that they get things done. Their voices ring out so
genuinely with St. Paul the truth that it is only when
they are weak that they are strong. It is only when
they acknowledged their need that they found their
strength.

Perhaps this is precisely the crux of the alchemy
of love—it makes one more aware of the beauty of
the gold in the rock than the crude stone surrounding
the precious metal. All those who are authentically
givers of the gift of the Lord view themselves far
more as receivers of gifts than as givers. It is they, in

their wondrous vision, who are recreated by the very ones to whom they would be of service. It is not a question of "come to me and I will make you better than you are." Such an all too common attitude has the same effect as leaving milk standing in the warm sun. Rather, the situation is, "I am sure in getting to know you I will discover a beauty I did not know before. And in this discovery, my soul will rejoice."

Were Sue to make Andy's acquaintance, she would feel herself fortunate indeed. Gift-givers do not see the world through the eyes of pirates, as a place full of plunder. They do not lay their hands on people or things that they might capture them, thus making themselves wealthy. Rather, they come upon the world as an artist, one who sees in reverence. One who would not snatch up but set free; one who does not first of all seek anything for himself, but rather glories in the beauty and meaning revealed in all things around him. They are people who do not first of all give but receive. They receive because they first of all experience themselves as needy. But only one willing to die to the ugliness in himself, can rise to a vision of the beauty in others.

There is immense power in receiving and being able to receive. What we all too often are strong in, is doing and taking pride in our ability to do. Thus we leave ourselves open to the tremendous danger of wanting to manipulate. We become so engrossed in an awareness to change all around us that we lose sight of the need to change ourselves. "Change" that translates evolving spiritually, becoming more than what we are by undergoing the journey of the grain of wheat. But this process necessitates that we become quiet and listen.

The Vacation

There was a man who took a winter vacation from a bitter cold northern city to a lovely Florida town. As he walked on the beach with his camera he took note of the many sea gulls. He noticed the tragic growth of acres of cement parking lots along the beach and gave up trying to count the neon-painted motel signs that all but concealed the gulf from any resident of the town. He noticed how many different license plates there were on various automobiles and laughed out loud upon seeing a car of college students with boxes, blankets, books and clothes piled up to the windows. He wondered how many times the sea gulls had been photographed and wondered what they thought of these strange humans continually pointing their black boxes at them.

Everyone seemed so busy except one man sitting quietly under a tree. He was the only one he could see who was not in a frantic hurry to capture relaxation. He wasn't doing anything but sitting there—looking, listening, receiving. What was he doing? Why wasn't he chasing fun? Who did he think he was anyway?

The vacationer sat down at a distance, put his camera and all the fun gear he had with him aside, and began to think.

"I feel the weight of this camera against my foot. Why do I have this camera? What am I trying to do? Am I missing something that quiet man under the tree has found? Perhaps this metal box is as much a sign of my handicapped spirit as a wheelchair or crutch is a symbol of bodily deformity.

"Perhaps like many (most?) of my fellow vacationers and those of my culture, I seek to have by possession. It is 'mine' when I can fence it in, own it, capture it. Ownership is rulership. Rulership is security. And security is the key to all good things. So the reasoning goes. But is this my reasoning?

"Perhaps that is why we kill all that we can. We kill the air, water and land to prove we have control over them. And thus we inherit graveyards. Is this what, in effect, I am trying to do with my camera? As an extension of myself I reach out through the lens and 'capture' the object. I would even capture the sea. Then I can take it back with me to do with as I please. I can show others, paste the pictures in my album, stow them in a drawer. But I am in control. With a sense of pride and superiority, I can boast, 'I have been there. I know that place.' Yet pictures or no—I haven't been there at all.

"Slowly I am coming to understand how poverty-stricken such an attitude is.

"I look at all the wonders around me and wonder, 'How do I become present to this place? How do I really come to know what is here?' One word comes back to me over and over again: listen. Listen with every ear of your being.

"Forget about capturing or controlling. Such attitudes are those of the spiritually deaf and blind who know nothing and are capable of learning the same. Listen, receive all that is being given. Let your skin hear the sound of the warmth, the feel of the salt. Be quiet and let the sand speak. Look with your inner eye until you see the Spanish galleon still bobbing in the bay. Listen with your eye to all that moves. We consider the birds cute as they perform their aero-acrobatics diving for food. Yet in reality they are struggling for survival. Just as the tiny sand crabs scurrying along the tide line.

"As complex as computers, the waves deposit their art in the wet sand. Forget about capturing it on film. Let it be. Let yourself become the tide and the sand. Join in the flow of what is. Enter in spirit to what this place is."

As the vacationer sat there watching the quiet man he mused a great many thoughts. "My body has occupied much space in many places. Few indeed, however, have I ever really been to. Seldom have I been still and listened. I was so intent on acquiring, on gaining, that the enormous power of passivity was lost. But to that quiet man sitting under the tree all things are revealed. To him who rushes around bear-like grabbing, collecting, clicking his lens, nothing is revealed. He has never been here at all.

"Wherever I go I shall ask myself, 'What did this place say?' Only then will I know if I have ever been there or not."

The next day the vacationer boarded a plane to return to his home. He didn't have many pictures to take back to show his friends and what he had to say of the place they wouldn't understand. How could you tell someone who wanted to know if you had fun or not, or what you got on your vacation, that he didn't get anything but the knowledge of the sound of waves and feel of sand? And very much the gift of a man who sat quietly under a tree saying nothing, doing nothing, and yet carrying on a most important venture.

Gift? Well, what did he give you?

The gift of silence.

They would think you were crazy.

We all would genuinely wish to change things for the better. But at times we fail to understand this means a willingness to become "crazy" enough to acknowledge the value of receiving, to know that we need to receive. Yet here is the whole underlying question of Jesus. Jesus frees—but do we truly want to be free? Christ is the Power. A Power delved into only by submission. Do we want to give up? Whose work is it we want to do—ours or the Lord's? If it is the Lord's, then why do we feel the outcome of our endeavors is contingent upon our power alone? If, indeed, the victory has been won, then why do I not let go and let it be?

Holiness admits of many degrees or levels. Perhaps the novice degrees are primarily those of activity, of doing. Either by actively doing these things or refraining from certain others we pass from areas of dimness to those of greater light. All necessary steps. Yet steps nonetheless leading somewhere else. Perhaps to the immensely more active areas of submission, the vast dimension of a Sue just sitting there, or the quiet man under the tree where things truly "get done," where the power is.

And anyone with eyes looks around and says, "Yes. Yes, it is happening but. . . ." We say we believe and yet continue to walk around in a semidark fog of despair. Repeatedly with the sisters of Lazarus we meet Christ outside the tomb, we hear Him ask us if we believe He has the power over death. We say YES but are very aware that immediately behind us yawns the grave holding our dead brother. "Yes, Lord, you have the power—but so does death."

Perhaps no one has put this dilemma of faith in

our time better than the celebrated Father Chardin, in his book, *Building the Earth*. ". . . No matter what reactions we may have to current events, we are first to re-affirm our robust faith in the destiny of man. Even if that faith is already there, it must be fortified. It is too easy to find an excuse for inaction, by pleading the decadence of civilization, or even the imminent end of the world. This defeatism, whether it be innate, or acquired, or a mere affectation, seems to me the besetting temptation of our time. Defeatism is invariably unhealthy and impotent; can we also prove that it is unjustified?"

He brilliantly and enthusiastically declares, Yes, it is unjustified. As a true believer in the Christ, he urges men to have hope. Yes, even hope in our time, which perhaps is far from the worst time in all of human history. We are alive now, gifted with this moment of time, privileged to mold the future to whatever form we will have it take. We project ourselves into the future from the present not as slaves who have no choice but to perish, but rather as the people of God, formed within the mystery of Christ. The battle has been fought. The blood of Christ has washed His people clean. We have risen with the Savior, if only we will die with Him.

PART II
THE GIFT OF HEALING

1. TRUTH

Would I be accused of unrealistic, fanciful poetry if I were to say that every minute of every hour, somewhere on this planet, a man is speaking the words of reprieve from mankind's death sentence? Over altars in every church, made of every material, some mud huts, some on the hoods of military jeeps, and one in the magnificent Basilica of St. Peter's in Rome, priests are saying, "This is the Lamb of God who takes away the sins of the world."

Rejoice! Sin *can* be taken away. The Power to embrace sin and evil and not die has become flesh among us. The rose has bloomed in our midst. And poetry is the deepest literary medium by which we can speak a human truth. The fact that God has loved mankind does not translate in a mathematical, analytical telling. It is poetry.

The light in Alice's face as Mike swings her in the air is poetry. The words "a man lifted a tiny deaf girl off the ground" says nothing of the truth of that scene.

"A man wrapped in the bindings of death walked out of a tomb four days dead" might be spectacular but it says nothing of the power, of the meaning of what went on. Who will put in words the beating of Martha's heart or the joy in Mary's mind? Who will capture in a cage of words what raced

41

through the skeptic's consciousness when Life was
called out of death?

It is a fact that a handicapped rodeo hopeful sat
on a floor with his eyes riveted on a woman deprived
of physical sight. That is a fact but it is far from the
total truth of the event. Words are not cages that
contain a meaning. They are lights pointing a direction in the darkness. What is emerging here is the
resurrected hope in the handicapped boy's heart.
What comes to mind is the awesome event of life-
giving Power leaping from one living temple to another.

"That's just poetry."

It is. It is also the most realistic way to attempt
a telling of a human truth. How else can one speak
of the angel that rose from Joyce's soul and caressed
her life as Roy proclaimed, "Girl, God don't make
junk."

The fact that in Christ man no longer need die
in his sin, is the stuff of the most profound poetry,
for it is the essence of what is most deeply religious.
Christ was not a lamb, but He was the meaning of a
lamb, the truth of sacrifice, who allows Himself freely to be led to slaughter, who bears in Himself the
marks of our malice.

If these pages are to be anything but an exercise
in delusion and an escape from an often problemat-
ical, painful world, we must understand Christ as He
confronts evil. Evil is too present and ugly to be denied. Crying out that the "Lamb of God has taken
away the sins of the world," must somehow realistically deal with that evil.

On a certain night not long after Christ had
transformed water into wine at Cana, a Pharisee

named Nicodemus approached Jesus. Nicodemus was toying with faith like a fish toys with bait. Tempted, but not ready to make it part of himself. John says Nicodemus was "a leading Jew," a big man in the community with much to lose if he followed Christ. But also with much power to lead others to life if he so chose. It would have to be his decision which direction his creative energy would go. He could scream and shout, "Crucify Him," as well as, "Brothers love one another." As easy as not, he could become a member of the blind, howling mob demanding blood, feeding on fear and hatred, as he could become a healer, an expeller of the demons of hate and fear. He would have to choose of which he wanted to become part: the community of faith and freedom, or to be eaten up by the mob. He, as we, could choose either.

Jesus claimed to be the Light. All that He did bore the marks of a man of vision. One who "spoke with authority." One who brought comfort to those in pain and joy to those who mourned. So obviously the man had some higher source of power and consciousness, so that it was said, "Jesus knew them all. He never needed evidence about any man. He could tell what a man had in him."

Nicodemus was a man in search of justification. Of some solid footing on and in a truth that this Jesus claimed to reveal and seemed to live. The Pharisee apparently was a man who had grown dissatisfied with the hypocrisy and shallowness of the life around him. There had to be something better, something more. If life was a wheel, he had found only half of it.

Immediately after humbly acknowledging that

Christ was of God, and shared in the power of God, Nicodemus hears a strange but challenging, statement from the Lord: "I tell you solemnly, unless a man is born again, he shall not enter everlasting life."

How did Nicodemus receive this? Here he was a dealer in law, not poetry. He was a practical man who concerned himself with what works or doesn't work, not with silly dreams and childish play on words. But this Christ was no dreamer. He was the man who had just driven the moneychangers from the temple, and that was no small task. People were flocking around Him in droves. He was working mighty signs, and there was great promise that He would do even greater things yet. But more important, there was always that light in His eye, that radiance that spoke of knowledge, but not of haughtiness; of kindness, but certainly not weakness; of strength, infinite strength, but not of the need to dominate. How should he respond to these words? Should he leave, chalking Christ up as a wild radical and this night as a waste of time? What should he do? What was this Christ talking about, "born again" to see the Kingdom of God?

Christ responded to this serious man's confusion with an unheard-of promise. A promise that would demand much of Nicodemus or anyone who would follow in the way. It would demand a trade, a barter of one thing for another.

Jesus told the Pharisee that what is born of flesh is flesh, but what is born of the spirit is spirit, and spirit alone will endure. All of Nicodemus' total doomed reliance on what is born of flesh must be traded away for what is of the spirit. It is the spirit alone that gives life, spirit that frees, creates, sings, and makes what is dead to live again. Only the gift of the rose transforms darkness into light.

But what of the law, the sacred law that has been with us since Father Moses returned from the mountain with the stone tablets, making us God's people?

". . . But I will give you a new law," says Christ, "a law born of spirit that will not settle as an unbearable yoke upon your hearts; one instead that will give you the freedom of the children of God."

And our sacrifice, what of that? What of the dense clouds of sacrificial smoke rising from the temple by which all people know we are pleasing to God?

"If you bring a gift to the altar and remember there that you have a grievance against your brother, leave it, and first be reconciled to him. Only then return to offer your sacrifice." When will you understand, says Christ, that God would rather mercy than sacrifice? What is born of flesh dies with the flesh. What is of spirit lives forever.

And the temple. What of the temple that has taken 46 years to rebuild? Is that also born of the flesh? "Tear it down, and in three days I will rebuild it."

Again, Nicodemus is mystified. How can this be? What unearthly thing is the Christ talking about? What strange unreal vision is Christ laying before him?

"We speak about that which we know," says Christ. "Yet, you people reject our evidence." As plainly as words can tell it, Christ is saying, He was not only speaking on His own authority, but there was one greater than He, the Father, and Christ was but handing on what the Father had given Him. The grand design, the truth of the quality and depth of the relationship possible between God and His people. Jesus was not speaking as one having an opinion among other opinions, but as one having authority, as the revealer of truth.

Jesus Himself was the Word. The Word made flesh full of grace and truth. A Word powerful with the very power of God, who alone offers to man the way of life. Jesus is the Word that calls all things from nothing, that creates, transforms what is flesh into its fullest and deepest meaning. Flesh revealing the spirit within. Christ as Word is the difference between a face that is locked in bitterness and hatred, and a face revealing the freedom and courage of the Son of God. It is the difference between a hand extended to strike and inflict pain, and one extended in friendship and welcome. Jesus as the Word is not only the ability to speak, but the ability to speak the spiritual reality of love and fellowship, that shouts into the darkness of human failure: don't be afraid. I am your brother; you do not have to fear me.

The Word who is Jesus calls life from the tomb. It confers the spirit, which is the source of immortality, and enables man to enlarge his awareness of himself to children of God.

Nicodemus must have sat there in wild-eyed amazement. What was all this? He had come seeking planks of philosophy, insights into a theology, and here this Carpenter possessed of such enigmatic power, was painting before him the landscape of unimaginable richness. He was asking this man of the law to widen the boundaries of his consciousness and deepen the rivers of his faith to a point that seemed impossible. The point to which Christ was taking him was so far into the darkness of his unexplored potential, that it was totally beyond him. Nicodemus was becoming a pilgrim in a completely new land.

"Yet you people reject our evidence." All that was required was that Nicodemus had faith in this Word who was Christ. Not a faith that relies on scientific certainties, such as the sun will come up in the morning, but a faith that allows one to actually dwell in the meaning of what is revealed. Faith that becomes the nourishment of the daily bread being eaten, that becomes the vision by which I see all that is in my world. Faith that is the strength, greater than my own, by which I not only endure, but creatively set about liberating the human spirit by the warmth of the Lord's touch in mine. Nicodemus was asked to do nothing but to abide in this word, which is power. To keep this word, which is truth. To obey this word, which is love, and in so doing, become the word who is Christ.

"If you do not believe me when I speak about these things in this world, how will you believe me when I speak to you about heavenly things?" Christ was washing over dazed Nicodemus like a tide. The word truly is given to all, but it is difficult. It makes its way only into humble hearts. Those who hear it respond in different ways. Some believe and accept the way. Others, regardless of all the signs of the spirit's wonder, go away darkly. Yet, it is this same word that judges day by day; this same power either accepted or rejected that is the measure of our freedom and joy.

We, of our advanced time, sit no different than

ancient Nicodemus. For us as well as the Pharisee, the Lord has offered unbounded dimensions to our living. If we but willingly submit, like Samson in the temple of his oppressors, the word comes into our lives, firmly planting itself against the pillars of our narrowness and foolish dependence upon our own power. And then the pillars move. They cannot withstand the power of the Lord. Our temple of idols comes crashing in to give birth to the living temple of the spirit, which shall never know destruction.

Nicodemus heard the Lord. He not only went away saying, "I know," but saying, "I am." He accepted the Carpenter's word, "The Son of Man must be lifted up, as Moses lifted up the serpent in the desert, so that everyone who believes may have eternal life." Jesus had to be lifted up. He must die. Evil then would conquer? Evil then and now? But why must He die; by whose decree?

"Yes, God so loved the world that He gave His only son, so that everyone who believes in Him might not be lost, but may have eternal life. God sent His son into the world not to condemn the world, but so that through Him the world might be saved."

Nicodemus had just heard Christ say that he, if he believe, was in Christ. Just as we are in Christ. Which again sounds like poetry; and again it is, for it is the truth.

The Son of Man had to be lifted up, and in the one magnificent breath of His life He drew inside of Himself all the evil, sin, failure and weakness of all men, and there He made it His own. The Son of Man was lifted up so that Nicodemus' sins and ours would lose their power. Once and for all, the Word achieved the victory, daily fought, daily won, of Christ's redemption over sin. The death and resurrection of Christ is more powerful than sin, more than yours or mine, more than our country's or our century's, more than *all* countries and *all* centuries.

The wider context is not sin and failure, war and hatred. Rather, these defects of men exist within the wider dimensions of Christ. Life does not exist as a thrilling but futile spark within the ultimate victory of darkness. Rather, death exists within the endless boundaries of Christ's renewed life. Nor is this a pious wish of man, or desperate dream of a dying race. It is truth spoken to us by the Word of God.

Center of Energy

Nicodemus had the option to cry out for Christ's blood, or proclaim Him as Savior. The center of energy for either was within him. Yet, on that day when the Hill of Skulls supported three crosses, Nicodemus was there as healer. He did not laugh as dice were rolled for the madman's clothes, nor justify the legal rights that brought the crucifixion to pass by quoting law to passersby. He had accepted the gift of dwelling within Christ, and he had faced the possibility of doing evil, and fully and freely chose to integrate and channel that possibility to creative goals.

The question of evil is the question of direction. Evil can exist only as an absence of direction, a failure to integrate all the powers that make us to be what we are and channel them toward growth. To be of God is to be in the process of becoming ourselves.

It is a matter of our own growth; of our spiritually evolving to be all we can be. Within each of us is immense potential. Roaming the often unfaced and unlit corridors of our souls are both our demon and our angel. It is not a matter of killing one that the other might live. To kill one is to destroy the other. The task is to, in the full light of consciousness, recognize our power, all that we are and can be, and choose which direction we would have that power take. Like Nicodemus, we are totally capable of screaming, "Crucify Him," or, "Be thou healed."

"I tell you solemnly, unless a man is born again, he cannot enter everlasting life." And the Lord, the Word who brings life from death and raises death to life, stands precisely at the center of each man's power. He takes His place within the framework of our spirits, our imaginations, our consciousness. Like a master gatekeeper at a mighty dam, His post is at that lever, that one wheel which opens or shuts the floodgates of our potential. The power is there. The energy which can either assume the evil, ugly face of violence and hatred, greed and lust, or the heroic dimensions of dignity and respect, kindness and strength. It is power awaiting the creative channeling marked by the gentle presence of the spirit, or rather stamped by the blind rampaging possession of unchecked forces.

As Nicodemus truly heard Christ and became ever more of the Lord, he was asked to go within and name his demon. Mighty deeds would be asked of this man, difficult things that would require that he be a free man. It is the demon in us that makes us slaves. All that is left unchallenged, unfaced, that would lead us in ways we would not go. If Nicodemus harbored a great fear of losing his position and following the Christ, he would have to name it, bring it to light, before he could deal with it and transform its direction to serve the Lord. If greed made him its slave or human respect, he would have to name that, as well. Perhaps pride was his stumbling block. After all, who wants to admit that he has been wrong?

And so with us.

Tony was only nineteen but already he was sure, "The world is doomed. People are mostly ugly and that ugliness comes to the surface with almost no provocation." What came to light was that, notwithstanding all the real uglinesses of the world, what Tony mostly thought was that he was doomed and he was ugly. His view of the world, like most of us, was primarily a projection of his view of himself.

But why would Tony feel this way? What horrid demon stalked the inner core of his temple peering out through his eyes, reaching out in his hands? What was the shield that so powerfully kept the poetic meaning of, "love one another as I have loved you" from pervading his consciousness, from melting the ice and causing the garden of his life to bloom?

"I am afraid."

Would you believe it was as simple as that. "I am afraid to fail. All my life I have been taught that besting the competition in all areas of life is the sole criterion of success. I hate competition; I hate fighting; and I am afraid I won't make the grade. We are not allowed fear in our family. Fear is weakness. My mind never stops shouting this; my heart can't stand it.

"Because I am afraid and fear is 'evil' I must be

evil. I feel shame for going against what I was taught
was 'good.' The more shame I feel, the greater my
guilt. The more the guilt, the more I know I am bad.
I am on a wheel spiralling downward with no direction to go but toward destruction. All is lost."

A few simple sentences. They are written so
easily—they were dug out and shared at immense
cost. And yet this evil demon possessing Tony's
mind bound him in the cruelest form of chains.
There would be, could be, no freedom until he faced
in the full terrifying light of consciousness what it is
he felt and was. There he could deal with it. Within
the context of a healing community he could face his
"evil enchanter."

Nicodemus had to face his demon or live as an
unliberated human being. And what of us? What has
the Lord called us to? "I am the truth, abide in me."
Truth that dispels darkness, demons and slavery al-
lowing one the thrilling adventure of human growth.

There is indeed a multi-faced demon doing a
brisk business in our time. Perhaps in every time. It
is a word spoken many different ways that says,
"You are ugly. You are doomed. There is nothing of
beauty in you." It spoke to Tony out of the context
of fear. It speaks to another in his seeming inability to cope with the pressures of life. It perhaps whis-
pers in the inner soul of another that, "You have
sinned. What you have done can never be forgiven.
You can never make it up to God."

BUT REJOICE! THE LORD HAS RISEN.
YOU DON'T HAVE TO MAKE IT UP TO GOD.
That is the fantastic, mind-shattering TRUTH, *God
loves you.* He has called you His own. You are not
an unclaimed sinner thrown on a cosmic trash pile.

You have been chosen, named, called forth by God in Christ that you may be free. And yet the lie persists.

We allow it to continue its false, enslaving existence among us, "I am nothing. I have nothing to give. I am devoid of gifts." So often to undertake an examination of conscience or moral inventory results only in finding suitable material with which to flog ourselves. We insist on emphasizing the flaws in our being and refuse to acknowledge all the unwordable beauty and goodness we CAN find within if we but look. We allow ourselves to see only the more or less closed, locked flower that we imagine ourselves to be and stubbornly decline to grasp to your hearts the essence of God Himself who has taken His place at the very center of our power. If only, like Joyce, all of us could hear in some powerful way the truth of Roy's words rumbling into our awareness, "God made you and He don't make junk!" The naming and dealing with our demon, again, is a matter of power.

Christ does have the power to expel demons. He does have the power over evil. Yet we, like Nicodemus, must name our demon. For only that person who "lives by truth, comes out into the light so that it may be plainly seen that what is done is done in God."

But here it becomes so difficult. To name our demon is, at the same time, to admit we want to deal with it. But do we? The ancient prophets who exposed to Israel the demons of pride, lack of trust, and infidelity were stoned. No one is overly fond of coming face to face with his power turned ugly. Yet to fail in the task of ghost-hunting is to guarantee our stagnation and insure our slavery. To believe that Christ has risen is to profess our belief there is no longer any need of slavery. There is power, unlimited power of which I can claim, enabling all of us to approach the table of the Lord with a gift, the gift of their demon named. Each in his turn could cast this tug to destruction on the Lord, to drown it in His love.

"Lord, I give you my fear. I am mightily afraid. I have reached middle-age, my physical powers diminish, my earning power is at its peak, my advancement will go no further. I am afraid of slipping, of losing the respect and love of my wife. I conceal this fear under the cloak of haughtiness and manipulation of others. Forgive me. Heal me."

"Lord, I am eighteen. I am confused. What is truth? What is right? Who is to say what is true and what is false? Which way to go? My confusion and searching have led me into dark, forbidding places. I do not know if I want to continue. Forgive me. Heal me."

"I have been your priest for many years. I have served you in good times and bad. Only you can count the times I served at your altar, ministering to your people. But now I am tired and worse, I no longer know if I believe. Perhaps I have looked too long into the face of mankind to believe that you are there. I do not want to lose you in the winter of my life. Forgive me. Heal me."

One by one they come. Fear, jealousy, self-pity, hostility—each casting in confidence and trust the gift of his weakness into the ocean of the Lord. Each trading the debilitating anchor of unnamed weakness for the freedom and strength of growth in Christ.

And so they gather. Those who in naming and dealing with their demons have found the strength to channel that power into the task of humanizing the earth.

2. HEALING

Christ plainly stated, "I have come not for the well, but for the sick." His invitation clearly was for all of those who were "weary and heavily burdened," that they come to Him and find rest. Jesus came not as judge to find fault, but as healer, who gently invaded the sick hollow of those souls whose demons had made life unbearable and had robbed it of all sweetness. It has been nearly 2000 years since the Galilean Carpenter whispered a mind-shattering secret into the circuitry of human consciousness: God is your Father; you are brothers, all of you; love one another; spread the word.

A problem appeared as the secret passed from one century to the next. A problem not with the secret itself, for it had never lost its power, but with the keepers of the secret. As with the glories of sunsets and snowflakes, people at times grew bored. Bored, blind and deaf. They said, "Oh, yes, we've heard that before. We've heard it all so often before." Generation by generation, the secret became identified with politics as in the time of the Spanish Inquisition; or with the nobility, as in the time of the French Revolution; or with the fierce struggle to stifle scientific learning, as in the time of Galileo. The secret came not to stand for a new way of life, but became synonymous with intellectual theory, magnificent processions, and even grander buildings. The

Carpenter's secret came to be the chief agent of security, which tolerated little or no spiritual evolution, rather than the restless urge to capture men's hearts which propelled a Paul, a John and a Peter along the dusty roads of the known world. The unstoppable energy, which in its depth of vision, forced a Francis or a Joan to wage war on the granite-like limitations of men's minds. But they did rage against those limitations, as has done every person touched by the spirit of God's power. All of them illuminated instead by the immensely complex, yet simple, secret: Love One Another. And in that love, heal those who are wounded.

"We have heard all that before. Tell us something new." And in so saying, we have made ourselves unable to receive the power of the secret. Just as the wonder of sunsets and snowflakes has no power to inspire those who, being too close, will not see. There is no greater need in our own or any other time than for the living of the secret of Jesus. Desperate beyond belief, we search for an answer. Some kind of computer-borne, science-reared logical answer, that will take us back again to at least the certain uncertainty of an age that will never return. Someday, maybe tomorrow, we think certainly someone will come up with an answer.

In our own time we have seen youth punish their own institutions of learning, soldiers shoot the students, and students hurl stones at the President of our country. We are being told what seemed impossible: that we are reaching the limit to growth. But there is only so much breathable air and its supporting eco-system fed by the oceans of the world, which we are destroying. Countless men in some nook or cranny of thought wonder, "My God, is it possible? Is it possible that in my time or my children's, our unbending hardness of heart will destroy the water and the air we need to live? Are we committing mass suicide?" Everything seems so involved, even for the most optimistic, the vision of "Man Progressing" dims. Yet, everywhere men hope against the dying of the dream. Frantically we search for an answer, a key, a restoration of sweetness to life, sanity to existence, serenity to our undertakings. When will we find the new discovery that will make everything all right?

And all the while, the haunting sad face of the Carpenter vaguely fades in and out on the rim of our consciousness, strangely reminiscent of a forgotten day when He sat on a hill outside His city weeping, "I would gather you under my wing." The answer, as much as there is an answer, is with us now.

Perhaps historians and philosophers of the future will write that our society's ultimate tragedy and blasphemy was that we paid so little heed to the "answer" that we had with us all the time. The secret that had become so familiar, so lacking in power to inspire, that we didn't even notice it was with us. Well might tomorrow's men shout back down the dead corridors of time to us, "The answer was with you all the time. Why didn't you use it?" Just as we could futilely, frustratingly, shout down the same corridor to men dying of infection: help is at your very fingertips in the mold of the bread you cast away from you. Pick it up, use it. Or just as vainly call out to shivering men dying of cold in the twilight of some prehistoric winter: warmth and light hide in the stones of flint lying all around you, pick

them up, use their magic. All to no avail. The magic
was not used. We could do nothing as we watched
infection become death and biting cold turn a body
to a corpse. But no, the tragedy was it didn't have to
be.

What does it mean to be healer: to carry forth
the mission of Christ who is love, into the world
around us?

Kay is the best street go-go dancer in a city of
over one million people. Her thin delicate face is as
impassive and non-committal as one of the ancient
brick alley walls in the downtown area where she
works. But her body pulses with flashing life, as a
broken high-power line blown down in a storm. The
face does not fit the body. It seems as if she was put
together by randomly selecting faces and bodies
from a catalogue, like putting a soldier's face on the
neck of a ballerina.

Her little window where she dances is like a
keyhole into which everyone walking or driving past
can peek. A car stops at a red light. Its middle-aged
righteous occupants fix their eyes firmly on the little
hole. Neither speaks, but their minds work furiously.
To the man she is a dish of ice cream and he, in his
mind, has the spoon. "She would love it. That's
probably all she lives for. Look at her up there,
wouldn't she be fun?"

The man's wife is far removed in her wordless
outburst of thought. "Tramp," she thinks. "Why
isn't she home loving her children. Children, that's a
laugh, she couldn't have any children. She wouldn't.
Immoral women like that can't love children or anyone else. They have no feeling. They don't care
about anyone.

"Nice legs, though," she thinks, as they pull away from the light. Secretly, deep in her unfaced self, she wonders how she would look in Kay's world. She hopes that she would look as good as the girl she thought so little of.

And Kay just kept dancing away.

Once away from her window, however, the face and body merge into one person again. One person who is not a go-go dancer, or showpiece, but a human being. One who has tears welling up from a depth many people never find. Kay's big problem is not that she is too tough, but not tough enough; it is not that she doesn't feel, but rather that she feels too deeply. Her great task now is to have the courage to reach for a sunrise, but her fear is so great.

Scalding tears boiled her face red, as she painfully recalled what was. Why had her first marriage turned so sour? Was it her fault? How hard she had tried. How much she had endured. It seemed to her that her duty, no matter how intolerable the situation, was to stick it out. And so she hung in there when Joe, her husband, had brought other women to the house. She put up with having to work hard for what he appreciated not at all, or gave away. The worse he was, the more she tried. It had all come to a head with the beating of the children. "Often," Kay tremblingly said, "I would hit the kids just so he wouldn't. He would make them bleed."

As vivid as if yesterday, she told of the time at work when he called and said he had beat the little girl. He told her not to get a drink of water. She did anyway. She was three years old. Kay came home. He told her hesitatingly that the baby was in bed. Her coming home had surprised him. But then Kay heard a whimper like a frightened dog, and there behind the door, stuck into the wastebasket like a piece of garbage, was her baby. Hatred, anguish, simply exploded from her. The whole scene was happening again.

My baby, just a piece of garbage, stuffed all bloody into a basket. Another page turned when she said the baby was not his. It was the product of her having been raped and beaten when she was nineteen years old, and yet out of that act of horrible insanity, came a pearl of beauty: the child and Kay's love for it.

She thought Joe "understood." Understood all that was involved. But can a flower bloom in a parched desert? Kay hungered for him to say that he loved her, just once in a while. To pull her arm or tease her, to make a face. All of those touching, human poetic ways that people in love tell each other they are there.

Kay, like a snake goddess, throbbed with life in her glass world. But her face was dead. All she had asked was a playful tug on the arm, a smile. At minimum, not to have her violent-born, gem-precious baby stuffed bloody and broken into a garbage can. ". . . girls like that have no feelings . . ."

Joe's parents were the architects of his sickness. No one gets that sick accidentally. During those five dark years they added their weight of poison. "Oh, forget it Kay, men are just like that." When she seemed ready to make a stand in favor of life by refusing to accept this unacceptable behavior, they accused her of not loving Joe because she would not forgive him. It was not their son's fault; it must be hers. Obviously, she was not enough woman to satisfy him.

Her eyes were as hollow as burned-out logs as she related how her parents were 45 years old when she was born. They never made it back to any kind of closeness after the act of giving birth to her. She never had anyone to talk to. No one standing with her when all the world was a hostile army marshalled on the opposite side of the ravine. She had no one to be at her right side and shout into her quaking soul, "They are wrong, so terribly wrong," when Joe's parents brought out their sickness, displaying it like an ugly cancer. And so, she wasn't quite sure if they were wrong or not.

As surely as professional thieves casing a place to rob for its weakest point, they soon found hers. The last resort in their madness was to shout, "You are crazy. We are going to have you put away, you are not safe." As alone and defenseless as Kay was, with no one telling her differently, and no wisdom greater than their sickness, she was trapped. In truth, she doubted her sanity, and with that doubt came total paralysis. Total inability to decide and, therefore, no power whatever to change anything for the better. An eagle who thinks he is a chicken will never fly.

The five years came to an abrupt halt. Her husband Joe was quickly killed in a car wreck. Kay took her battered children, whom she knew were injured far more in spirit than body, and left. Eventually to find the glass keyhole. With her, as certainly as her luggage, were countless bloody holes blown in her consciousness. Was she crazy? Even though she had poured every ounce of her love into the marriage, was it somehow, somehow, her fault, that it had ended so brutally? Maybe she was simply unable to love. Maybe in some strange divine economy she was simply put here by God to suffer and to lose. Could she possibly raise her children? Would they find the same vicious, ugly world she had? Would her baby ever, in all her life, ever get out of that garbage can? Would her whimpers ever cease? And if not, would it be Kay's fault?

Kay is not yet close to 25 years old. She dared not even think of possibly having happiness or anyone treating her with any measure of respect. That was not possible. Bag and baggage she headed north.

But a day came she never thought possible. A man named Mark found and loved her. Mark is a man who can love and, therefore, it is credible. Love that knows more than mere outer form. What Mark loves is the look of joy on the kids' faces when he plays with them. He bursts with quiet happiness to see Kay's face gleam as they tease each other and finger one another's souls. He loves the things of which love is made. And now there they stand, facing a new dawn. Can they walk to it? Perhaps. So many ghosts possess her spirit. So many long ago visitors howl through her mind at night. So many questions still unfaced and unresolved. Can Kay rise above all the demons pulling her back? Can she believe she is worthy of a decent life? Will Mark's love and maturity be deep enough to tolerate the wounds until they are healed? Will either one be tough enough to make a go of life?

Grind away dead-faced girl in your glass window. Let everyone think what they will about who you are or are not inside your lovely body. A group

of people once brought a woman, perhaps her face
too did not match her body, before Jesus the Healer,
as He sat trying to dispense warmth upon ice. They
said she wasn't much of a woman either. Jesus
thought quite differently. Herein lies the mysterious
power of healing. Jesus thought differently. A different light shone in His eye. Every word He spoke
was a different word.

The Touch of Christ

John himself tells us that every book in the
world could not contain all that Christ did and said.
Which is not important. For what we have does
communicate sufficiently to reveal who He was.
Lover. Free enough to love, brave enough to care,
strong enough not to be threatened by others'
strength, tall enough to stoop to all tiny people, wise
enough not to despise their ignorance. Perhaps in
view of this we don't have to know all that Christ did
or said. But my, what stories could have been told!

Scripture tells us that He cured a man born
blind. It says nothing of the tone of His voice on this
occasion. Nor the look on His face when He touched
the sightless sockets. Yet healing change issued every
bit as much from this inner light of Christ as from
the power to convert non-functioning eyes to seeing
ones. Often we hear that Christ cured the sick far
into the night. That from far and near they brought
their ill to Him. "And He laid His hands on all of
them."

Oh, but nothing is said of the gentleness of that
touch. No word tells us of the pain registering in the
sky of His countenance as He looked upon every

manner of ill known to that time. Did He weep when
the legless teen-ager was brought before Him? Weep
as He knew this young adult would never dance, run
or climb? How badly did it show that He wanted to
take this human being in His arms and hold him till
it all went away. Yet knowing it would not.

The parents of a crippled infant—how deeply
did their anguish and hope bore into His spirit?
What vibrations poured from the Lover as He leapt
into the bottomless lake of their hurt? I wonder how
tenderly He touched hunched backs, twisted arms,
bent legs; how eagerly His eyes devoured the pain of
these, His beloved people, as He spoke of healing.
Did those accompanying Christ sense that literally
He was eating them, taking them all inside Himself,
drinking their poison and neutralizing it in the ocean
of His goodness?

Contemporary medical skill could have, perhaps
some might argue, heal all those Christ touched. Yet
medical skill could do not a thing to change them.
To eclipse bitterness, eradicate hate, sweep consciousness clear of obstacles is the province of love.
Only love and lovers can effect the radical change of
re-creation.

Zachais is a familiar name to all Christians. A
success story of the first magnitude. From far down
the road of greed and materialism he was won back
to himself. The Lover opened a door and he entered.
Force could have altered his behavior. But only love
could have changed his spirit. Christ must have experienced extreme joy at Zachais' reception of His gift.
Yet not a word is said of the countless other Za-
chaises who did not. What was the quality of sadness
flooding His eyes, etching its withering lines in His

sensitive face as He watched them walk away. He knew where they were going, yet could not stop them. Though His heart would break, He could not stop them. For love can only invite, never demand.

How many of those long nightly vigils were spent in sorrow over those who freely chose not to be free? Nights such as when He wept over the city of Jerusalem. A city that was a gleaming gem set squarely on the band of centuries of prophecy. Christ knew that city would be destroyed. How tenderly he reached out to all of them. For they, His people, were first. Above His own comfort, advancement or even safety. Before all He cared for them. And so only as liberator could He be man of change. But to liberate is to love.

"With great sadness," says Matthew, "He watched the rich young man turn and leave, for He loved him." What is the stuff of "with great sadness?" No force in the universe is more powerful than authentic concern. It is violent. Christ violently loved the young man and all the Mary Magdalens selling their birthright for pottage. Such agony must have boiled within Him at their conditioned blindness. He willed that they would walk in the light. As those parents are crushed but helpless as they witness their children choose death over life. Jesus desired their freedom, which is a matter of inner choice.

His reaching out for others was not even eclipsed by the climax of His greatest physical pain. Christ met the women of Jerusalem and communicated concern to them even while He was in the process of being murdered! He cared more about what was going to happen to them than what was happening to Himself. To the end, He was Lover. The beloved before all and above all.

Who is Christ? Renegade, rebel, hero, superstar? Perhaps all are true, perhaps none. What is true is that Christ loved. All else flowed from that. Overlook love and you have eliminated the essence. To justify our own behavior by saying this is what Christ did, may miss the mark entirely. Let us first acknowledge that all the Son of God did was motivated by love and was a perfect reflection of that motivation. He never acted out of vengeance or any base motive; one thought—to set His people free. To enable them to walk in human dignity, away from the ever-present lure to revert back to the jungle so close behind us.

We have many intelligent men in our midst today. Many who are wise in the ways of things. There are those who have the ability to make buildings rise almost to the sky, and those who have the gift of making a dollar of every dime that passes through their hands. There are those who can make us laugh and cry, and those who make us think. Our prophets and artists make us aware of ourselves and our times.

So many have so many gifts. All are needed. But perhaps there are none more essential in our, at times, unlovely times, of such great fear and confusion, as those with the gift of healing. Those who assure us, who desperately need to be assured, that love *is* possible.

3. COMMUNITY

Christ deals with the fact of evil, which is a question of the possibility of channeling our energies toward certainty or destruction, on two levels, both leading one to another. First, He calls everyone to an integrated creative life made possible by the conscious awareness that He, as healing Love, is with us. His power is our power. In all truth, Christ has "pitched His tent among us."

Secondly, however, from the very beginning, this process called holiness was to take place within the context of a believing community. To be of Christ is not of the nature of a momentary, brilliant illumination. It is not an instant thrill, as a shooting star streaking across the midnight sky. These moments of thrilling spiritual clarity may occur. But the nature of the Way who is Christ is a journey. It is a continual day after day discovery of who I am, and who the Lord is among us. The naming and taming of the demon in our hearts or society is no easy task. In fact, its demands are so rigorous that without the support of a believing community the journey most often will end or never begin.

We need the communion of consciousness, the breaking of the bread of faith with one another, if we are seriously attempting to daily progress beyond

our own comfort zone. Like Nicodemus, we are
called to celebrate life in our rituals, not merely perform them. We, just as those who listened to Our
Lord on the grassy slopes of Palestine, must be
growing to that point where we will understand that
it simply does not make sense to bring our gift to the
temple knowing we have unforgiven anger in our
hearts against our brother. For we know that *we* are
the gift brought to the Lord. Anger is a demon that
must be faced. Only dead men have no need of community, a community that not only supports but
challenges and inspires.

The immensely powerful, thrilling challenge of
Christianity today is not only to become conscious
of our own potential, but to acknowledge the healing
power of our Christ-centered communities. We are
the means whereby Christ has chosen to confront the
evil of the world.

At times some of the most deeply fundamental
of human interaction is clearly seen taking place in
the midst of youth. It isn't that these human feelings
and involvements aren't happening on other levels of
life; it is just that in youth they seem so much more
obvious.

A poet once said that the totality of fall can be
seen in the brilliant, dying color of a single leaf. He
said the complexity of the cosmos is revealed in a
single atom and all the sweetness of humanity can be
seen in a single child's innocent face. So it was that
an expression of universal worldwide need and healing took place within the context of some fifty senior
high school students on an evening of recollection.

This was a follow-up of a weekend retreat with
these students. Sue, Terry and many of the people

you've met in these pages were gathered together. We had worked very hard on this weekend to help the students "go in," to find themselves and not be afraid to see and acknowledge who they were. We wanted them to name their demons and their angels. Now we were shooting at something else.

This evening we wanted a spider web of solid, spun gold to begin forming between them. We wanted the priceless quality of freedom to pour out of their spirits and begin to reach out to and touch each other. We wanted them to grow in consciousness, extend their gift of healing to each other. Or, in other words, we wanted a genuine, Christian community to begin to form. It happened like this:

Each of the students was given a lengthy questionnaire to fill out. The questions dealt with their own attitudes and feelings. The young people were to take up to an hour writing out as honestly as they could their present stance toward their parents, home, school, church, their attitudes on the more pressing moral questions that confront them. There were many probing questions on just who Christ was to them and if they truly believed in His power to free them.

It was stressed that their answers would not be shared, no one else would read them. In fact, a large fire was built and the point was made that right then and there all the questionnaires would be burned. This was done in an effort to encourage honesty, to force all the demons and angels to appear.

When the last student had finished, the long line started filing up to burn their soul-in-writing. Before each one burned his papers, however, he was invited to share with the group one thing he hoped to change or deal with as a result of doing the exercise. It started slowly.

One shy, quiet girl named Gail almost whispered, "I have to try to trust you," and threw her paper in. We discussed a bit what the group heard. Why was she afraid of them in the first place? What made her afraid? What response did the community have back to Gail? They began to acknowledge their power of healing the demon of fear which had such a grasp on her spirit. They were the ones she was afraid of.

Don fairly shouted, "I must try not to be such a hypocrite." Why did he feel that he was a hypocrite? Because there was so much peer pressure on him to be what he wasn't. So much was expected of him that he felt most unfree to be what he was. How did the community hear what he had to say? They and they alone had the key to the door which, if Don would pass through, would bring him to his own Promised Land.

June said, "I must try to regain my faith in the Church. I think it is a lie. It says one thing, but is another." Like what? Like a praying community. June shared with the Church present right there that she felt there was no concern in the "Church." It was all talk. Where would June find the power to believe? Who could speak to her of the truth of what the Church was? All of the fifty students would see June the next day at school. What would they do? What would they say? Would they even recognize the fact that she was there? What does it mean to heal?

Lorri simply said, "I need support for a great decision I have to make." She never said what it was. But we didn't have to know. The fact was she didn't want to have to make it alone. She alone could follow whatever path she was talking about, but she did want to know someone cared. Who else had the power to effect this change if not the group right there?

And so it went for over an hour. Some more or less honest. Some dealing with home situations, some with personal problems related to narcotics, some personality problems. Each one had to face his own demon, but each needed the support and strength of an authentic, healing community of faith if the decisions made that night would have any lasting effect. Shooting stars are spectacular, but shed little light. What was needed was a slow, steady dawning, leading to noontime. And that process demands the effect of Christ's words, "Love one another."

There have always been two dimensions of a Christian's process of "conversion of heart." One is forgiveness of wrongs and the other is healing. We have put much stress on forgiveness, but have dealt lightly with healing. Perhaps because we can cast the responsibility of forgiveness on the Lord. "God forgives" comes easily to our lips. Healing becomes much more our responsibility. All the wounds resulting from failure to accept and recognize our own lovableness can only be healed by one standing without and knocking long enough until the door is opened. Before that door is opened, however, anyone who stands without will be tested. If the Healer's strength is not deeper than the wounded's weakness, there will be no healing.

If Gail is to overcome her fear, it is ourselves

who must embrace that fear. If Don and June are to be healed, it is the Community of Christ, in His name and with His power, who must submerge them in their corporate strength if they will be whole. Yet the strength of healing comes from the act of dying as wine issues from the crushing of the grape. From our viewpoint, it is easier for Christ to forgive than it is for ourselves to heal.

And yet that power is there.

It is unclaimed power, unclaimed for it never occurs to us to claim it, that permits so much evil to exist in our world. We are able through the power of Christ to evolve past our wildest dreams. Jesus has claimed us as His own. We have but to claim the Lord. Our communities not only *could*, but have been called forth *for* the very reason of healing. But this scarcely can happen if our Christian communities are not operating on the level of life and death. If they are not aware of their spectacular position as "answers" to the problem of evil in the world, how easily to blindly go about our business of routinely acting our rituals, of saying all our religious words, all the while missing the point of the power we have to rechannel the destructive energy that flows within us, thus liberating ourselves and our suffering brothers.

Dr. May makes the point that "not to recognize the demonic itself turns out to be demonic. It makes us accomplices on the side of the destructive possession." Yet, how foolish a minister would be considered if he rose before his people and said something to the effect that, "There is a great deal of power among us this day. Power that tends to be used to destroy rather than build. We must chose the direction. Either way hurts, yet in one case the pain is that of withering, leading but to the tomb. The other is the pain of birth, of creation. Each of us can contribute to the life of the world. We are houses consisting of many rooms. Some of those rooms may have dark, unlit corners in which hide our own personal demons. We are here to confront those demons in the name of the Lord and in the presence of one another. We need not fear to do it alone. We are here to celebrate life by confronting death. No one need fear, for no one does it alone."

Surely sitting in every congregation is a young Wendell. Next year this boy will graduate from high school. He is a loner, total and complete. Not long ago his parents split up, a natural result of the direction their lifestyle was going. This crushed the boy. His fear is monumental. His trust is non-existent. He has pulled the walls in around him and lets neither himself out, nor anyone else in.

Beside him sits tiny Allison. One of the sweetest teen-age girls who ever lived, except that she is messing around with narcotics. She also feels herself a loser. For some reasons, which are truth to her, she never received the love and recognition at home she craves so desperately, especially from her father. She is wise now. Wise enough to know how to manipulate her family. Her negative behavior at any time she chooses will bring the house down. But it is all around her, and that is what she wants.

To be sure, the decisions to be made are theirs. No one can burst through the doors of their minds making the decisions for them as to the direction of their lives. But we may ask are we, as a community of redeemed love, aware of our power and responsi-

bility toward one another? Both Wendell and Allison
have been baptized, which is to say initiated into a
community who in turn has the brilliant sun of
Christ at its center. The Christ who continually casts
out demons, freeing the power of the tormented
brothers and sisters, so they could be creative builders of the kingdom.

We are the community which Wendell and Allison need to fight their demons. But not only them.
Look around at any gathering at any liturgy. There
is John, whose advance to middle-age inspired the
demon naming of fear. Wendell and Allison are the
confused youth, whose efforts at freeing themselves
have led them into such desperate places. And yet
perhaps the very priest celebrating that liturgy is the
same man who in the quiet of his room prays for the
faith he fears is slowly slipping away.

It is not necessarily that any of these should or
must shout out to the community the nature of their
demon. The point is the level on which the community is living. Is it on a level of life and death? The
level of Lazarus, of the Lord bringing life out of
slavery? Is there a willingness to face death or our
own destructive tendencies, knowing the community
will be there? What is the meaning of the sacrament
of reconciliation, or baptism, or the sacrament of
union in Eucharist, if it is not a way in which we
hear ourselves say, "This is my demon. And understand that I am forgiven by my God and supported
by my brothers. That we are together in our efforts
to become whole." We can be sure that among our
community there exist a John, and an Allison, and
a great many others in need of our help and support,
speaking their souls in inviting our help.

Structures Perpetuating Evil

What is to the point of this discussion is the question of awareness. An awareness that leads to the conscious effort to be of aid and healing power in and through my community. In and through all the external signs we so familiarly avail ourselves of.

But this same consciousness makes us aware of the fact that we, as individuals, are not the only sources of evil in the world. To seriously confront the pain, suffering and human failure of this world is to take seriously the structures from which much of this evil comes.

It is one thing to have a war end, and it is quite another to reverse the processes whereby war is allowed to exist in the first place. It is one thing to provide welfare and poverty programs of all kinds, and quite another to seriously undertake the renewal of the structures, whereby the need for the poverty for which the programs were initiated, exist at all. It is one thing to allot the American Indian so much funding and assistance to catch up with the rest of the country, and quite another to seriously confront the whole question of reservations and the conditions under which they exist. It is one thing to vote and raise our voices against crime and the need for law and order, and quite another to consider the conditions out of which those who commit the crimes and break the laws come.

If we are to take the words of Vatican II seriously that, "The joys and the hopes, the griefs and the anxieties of the men of this age, especially those who are poor or in any way afflicted, these are the joys and the hopes, the griefs and the anxieties of the followers of Christ. Indeed, nothing genuinely human fails to raise an echo in their hearts," we are compelled to not only increase our consciousness of the purpose and meaning of Christ with us in our rituals and liturgical assemblies but also to address ourselves to the wider community where our brothers are starving for lack of both physical and spiritual bread.

One of my duties nearly ten years ago was a weekly one hour session with "residents" of a teen-age detention home. It was an easy ten-minute walk from where I lived. To arrive at the door to the detention center, one had to walk first alongside the fenced-in, barbed wire yard attached to the center. This was the child care unit. Here were abandoned kids, wards of the state, some of them not yet old enough to walk with much self-confidence. The clientele of this unit was up to nine years old. Even though they lived behind barbed wire, they weren't criminals—they just had nowhere else to go.

Anyone walking by when the children were out in the yard was soon to have his heart broken, especially if the children knew you. They would come to the fence as fast as they could toddle, crawl or scamper, squeezing their fingers through the triangle, cyclone fence for anyone, ANYONE, to shake them, play with them, just touch them.

Frequently, the older ones would tie their shirts into a knot and using it as a ball, play catch with whomever would play with them the whole length of the fence. "Hey, Mister, catch." If you dared stop, there would be immediate conversation. Where do you live? Where are you going? Do you have any kids? What do you do? How old are you? SEE ME,

SEE ME, SEE ME. I AM HERE!

At the end of the walk was the door to the teenage unit. "Criminals." Some were being held for felonious assault, some for armed robbery, some for prostitution. No doubt today there are many held on drug charges. Some were in for rape and some for stolen cars.

Only the hardest heart would not be torn at the pitiful scene of tiny children behind barbed wire fences playing catch with knotted shirts, with anyone who happened along. The sight of grasping, love-starved fingers reaching for all they are worth through the openings of a fence for someone to take them, is enough to prompt one to tears.

But what of the other scene? What of the hardened eyes of their older brothers and sisters? What of the hostile, cynical responses of their conversation? What of all that negative behavior that got them there?

Yes, they are the ones who stole your car, beat up the old man, robbed the store. And where did they come from? Yesterday they were begging for someone to but touch their fingers. What seems like only hours before, they were in the next door yard pleading for someone to whom they could throw their shirts. There was no cynicism, hatred for authority, cruelty then. They could hurt no one, so were not taken all that seriously. That was then, now is now.

Now they can hurt. They are a threat, a danger. They are liable to punishment and detention. But it didn't have to be. The old man's head didn't have to be caved in, nor the storeowner bludgeoned. If someone would have heard their call soon enough, some

Christian who understood the meaning of, "I baptize you in the Name of the Father, Son and Holy Spirit," some believer in the victory of Christ, who felt deeply enough in his heart, "I have made you fishers of men," it wouldn't have had to happen at all.

More fundamental yet—the question is cast not only in terms of preventing others from getting hurt, but these children did not have to be so cruelly broken. There never had to be that blasphemous slide downhill of those precious, never-to-be repeated children begging for someone to notice, to touch, to heal. It didn't have to happen if. . . .

If the millions upon millions of Christians forming into thousands upon thousands of communities who understood that to worship is to heal, would not allow it. If, claiming the Power of the Lord, they would so respect life that they would challenge the countless tombs of death that honeycomb our world.

Yes some, many, would say this is but ineffectual, pious theory. It just doesn't work because people aren't that way. As long as men have been men there have existed the processes borne of hardness of heart which dehumanize and desecrate our fellow man. Ever since the very dawn of human civilization some five thousand years ago the tide and eddies of life have been regulated not by cultural advancements but by war. Armed men burning and murdering their fellows have created the significant milestones marking the totality of history. What a Christian has to say of "healing communities" might be nice and in certain, unimportant instances, it is successful. But it just is not practical. It is not life as it is.

Practical? What is practical? What is reality? Is

it reality that a Gail, Don, Mary and Joyce should live their lives in the gloom of slavery? Is that life as it is? Must we submit to that indignity? Is that the way it has to be? Is not the possibility of healing as much "of life" as those processes that destroy?

To be sure, the tiny children behind the barbed wire fence might very well grow into the "criminals" of another day. Many will not "make it" to any kind of decent, productive life. But there is an option, an answer, if we will but avail ourselves of it. And the frightening, responsibility-laden truth is Christ has picked us, our communities, to be that answer.

PART III
THE GIFT OF FUTURE

1. CREATION

A pilgrim people seeking a new home wearily arrived at the shores of a vast lake. They found the lake inviting. Decades ago they had been driven from a far place because they found their beliefs and their values incompatible with those among whom they lived. Being different, they were considered dangerous and being considered dangerous, they were driven off.

But now they found their home. They looked around until they found a suitable place by the lake, and then set about constructing buildings, making laws, initiating traditions. Their buildings, laws and traditions they were sure would never mirror those of their former city, for those had been too rigid, inflexible. This new people were sure that theirs would be different. They would have room for all.

As years slipped by, their buildings became taller, their laws more complex. When one of their number would push out a little onto the lake in a canoe, they would remark how fine and large all their buildings looked. The tradition that grew out of living life as they found it began to be lived for the sake of the tradition, rather than for the sake of the life that was being lived. More years passed by.

New young faces began to appear in the city, the children of the travelers. They had no part in constructing the buildings they found as part of their living. They had no voice in making the laws. The tradition that had aged to steadfast certainty grew out of experience that the children had never known. But they were told tradition was good, even that it was sacred. Uneasiness appeared for the first time.

The older people remembered in the dawn of their youths a similar feeling. But, they said to their souls, that was different. Those laws and traditions were unfair, they were unchangeable. Ours are sacred, for we have made them.

A new word was brought back to the community's consciousness: crime. It had not been used in decades. The youth had never heard of it before. They did not understand its meaning, especially when they were accused of committing this crime. The old ones said it was a crime to question, a crime not to hold as sacred what they did, a crime not to say yes to what has always been called good, even though "always" extended back only to the time of the establishment of the new city. And with crime came trials.

The young people could not believe what was happening. One of their number, their freest spirit, was taken from their midst. He was accused of one of these crimes. The crime was that of leading others astray. He could not understand, "Away from what?" All he did was see things and ask, "Why?"

They killed the young man and all the old ones said what a pity that he had committed this crime. What a pity he could not be like the others, that he could not understand.

The next day the city was empty of young people. Everyone awoke to find that they had gone. No one knew where they went. Some said they had been seen walking down beside the lake. Others said they had all been criminals and it was good they were gone. Still some, the very wisest, knew in the inner storeroom of their memories, where they had gone, for their spirits had at one time walked the same path.

Many miles from that city a new people, without a home, walked a shore of the same vast lake. They, in their time, had been the ones driven out by buildings and laws and traditions that had grown too rigid for spirit, too complex for change. They, like their parents before them, made a solemn promise on the spot of their new city, that this time it would be different. In their new society there would always be room for what was important. Life would always be the primary and most important priority. Things would not become ends unto themselves, even if those things were the very laws by which the people live. And they settled down to wait a new dawn and the challenge of their parents.

The parable is obvious. All renewal and growth takes its stance in the present, but looks toward the future. The question is: Will the sins of the past be visited upon the future by the sons of today? The question is: Will we make available to our children the attitude and vision of Christ's victory, so that they may creatively, humanly, cope with the world they will inherit? And not only cope with the world, but create it in the image of their God.

Everyone, every culture, every era, began construction of a new city with mighty vision and certitude. It would be different, better. Structures would be malleable. Laws would be agents of freedom, rather than oppression. Traditions would always be open-ended, open to the experience of the people from which tradition grows, never would tradition become an end unto itself. So the dream goes.

It is essential, as we proceed to the final section of our discussion of the meaning of Christ, that we consider the future. It is our responsibility. We shall initiate the future for our children, just as today was initiated and prepared for us by those who went before. The basic element involved when a true believer considers the future is his fundamental understanding of time yet to come. He may either see it as a cycle endlessly repeating itself, predetermined, fixed, not truly subject to man's influence or power to change it. Or he may view the future as unknown, undiscovered and uncreated. That is, basically unfinished as yet. Being uncreated, it awaits for the people who will put hand to it and make of it what they will. Either it will be formed into a mechanical repeat of yesterday, or it will boldly look forward to the progressive reshaping of the earth under the imprint of the spirit. And this renewing of the face of the earth is what Christ is all about.

Those who view the future as cyclical or merely repetitive see life yet to be lived as predestined. It is as yet in the dark awaiting the light of the present to bring it into view. But since it is already completed, we have little or no part in forming it. Some huge force greater than ourselves has set the wheels in motion and they cannot be altered or stopped. An individual's part to play in such a view of the future is simply to be patient and wait for the future to happen.

However, those who see the future as basically uncreated take a totally different stance toward the future, which means a different stance in the present. Being uncreated, it calls out to my responsibility to make of it what I will. And if it is a stale repeat of yesterday dragging all the old sins into the sun of the present, then it is not fate which is to blame, nor is it merely God's responsibility, but my own lack of courage to face the challenge as a thinking being and give life to the spirit.

If the future is cyclical, then there really is not much sense worrying about it, for it is already completed. Spiritual growth, therefore, becomes a game, for we have no power to change what will be. If, however, the future is basically uncreated, then it must be my prime concern. Christ, in the light of this view of the future, becomes the source of energy, demanding courage, hope and faith in His victory over death. Christ demands fortitude of His believers to risk such an immense task as taking our stand in the creation of what will be. For this is exactly the question: What will be?

The fabric of tomorrow is the fabric of today. A believer can only bring to the process of creating tomorrow that which is being created in himself this moment. The future is a matter of the healer asking: "What in me is worthy of living into the future?" One who would be healed and a healer of the pain of his fellow man must see the future as basically unfinished. Basically waiting for the power of the touch of one who cares enough to eradicate as much pain and suffering as possible from the human community. He must see the future, existing within the context of Christ's victory over death, as possible of something much better than it has been today. We are aware of the saying: the radical of 18, is a liberal of 25, the progressive of 30 and the conservative of 40. Like all sayings, it is open to various interpretations. But if it means like the opening parable that with the passage of years comes the hardening of spiritual arteries so that structure is endured for the sake of structure, tradition as an end unto itself, and law as sacred because it is law, then we have allowed history to be a pitiful repetition of past sins. The fault and the crime of failing the future is everyone's who allows what is not worthy of life to live into tomorrow. The blasphemy is that of fear. Fear to look deep within the vast potential of my own creative abilities and ask, "What is worthy of life, for that which lives will be tomorrow?"

Any demon of hate, prejudice or refusal to open the doors of our temples, must die. For in living it sets in motion the process whereby children as yet unborn will be forced from their homes by the conservatives of 40, who themselves were orphans of a younger time. It is not possible to fail the future if we do not fail the present. The same truth is that today's victory of the spirit is the guaranty of tomorrow's freedom.

If the saying, however, means that as years progress so does the wisdom which most effectively allows the spirit to be born, it is a wonderful saying indeed. For wisdom, unlike mere intellectuality, necessarily speaks of and grows from the lived situation. It is wisdom that allows man to know when it is time to be quiet and when it is time to speak. When it is time to sit and when it is time to march. When it is time to bear witness by furious activity and when by the sword of silence. Wisdom allows one who would be a healer to discern which time indeed it is. For wisdom is the flower of love and love offers the only vision whereby a man correctly sees.

Perhaps the greatest gift of wisdom is the certain grasp of the paradox that indeed I am the future but not the whole of it. I am tomorrow, but only one hour of its life. My total responsibility is only for my own projection into the future, yet all men today and yet to be born are also growing in my garden awaiting for my tending. The gift of wisdom allows the man to take the present and, therefore, the future with immense concern, yet with humor; to see the multiple unspeakable evils of today, but also the undeniable springs of spiritual awakening; to confront suffering but also rejoice in brotherhood; to condemn death but affirm life. There is a paradox here. A paradox that is absolutely essential for one who would be a healer in the name of Christ to grasp. If he does not take himself seriously, then he cannot take his role in the future seriously. But if he takes his role in the future as the ultimate condition for spiritual victory, then he is as blind as the man who thinks that spiritual growth can be stopped.

The saying is open to various understandings. We must believe that the future is not complete. It calls out to each man for his donation to its ugliness or beauty, its slavery or freedom. The future is ours. Its condition depends on the amount of spiritual reality I am willing to give birth to today and allow to grow into tomorrow. There is no folly greater than thinking, "The future will take care of itself," or saying, "My part is ultimate in the decision of tomorrow."

Tomorrow may or may not find the city "empty of youth." It may or may not already be empty of youth. If it is, it is because we have allowed what is unworthy to live today and may very well do so tomorrow. If we have failed the present, and therefore the future, it is because we have not availed ourselves of the victory that Christ has already won over sin and death. It is not just a matter of new or the old having its way. Neither one is sacred. It is a matter of the spirit, which is truth and love, to be allowed to live and grow. The old has no more claim on it than the new. Only he has a claim on the spirit who allows the spirit to possess him.

Future As Mystery

There are those who look upon the future as a problem, a problem that admitting of enough accurate data lends itself to answers. Everything can be answered. Poverty or wealth, peace or war, ecology or pollution, life or death, are all problems. Truly difficult, but nonetheless problems, and every problem has an answer.

Every problem *does* have an answer. The future does admit of many problems, but more than this. The future is also a mystery, and when a mystery is reduced to the level of a problem, it cannot be faced, dealt with, or allowed to grow. When a man facing a beautiful sunset curses the sunset because of its lack of light, he views it as a problem, a problem that needs to be solved. But when the man faces the sunset as a beautiful experience and rejoices in the marvels of God and nature, he views it as a mystery. A man who looks at a magnificent tree and curses it because it is standing in the middle of his field and needs to be cut down and removed so that the business of planting be gotten on with, views that tree as a problem, a problem that needs to be solved. But when that same man can view the same tree as a glorious thing, as a truly wonderful example of life, then he views it as a mystery. At times children definitely are problems. How do you feed, clothe, house and educate them on seemingly not enough resources? But when a person looks at his children and sees the continuation of the human race before him, sees the vast potential of life or death growing in them, notices and marvels and wonders at the growth of intelligence and wisdom, then he is viewing those children as mysteries, not problems.

Mysteries have no answers admitting of sufficient data. They have no answers at all. For one of the elemental segments of data concerning mystery is that it basically always has infinitely more to reveal than is shown. Mysteries admit to imagination, wonder, pride and quality of life as well as quantity. Mystery deals not in percentages, but in awareness; not in profit but perception; not in deals but growth; not in business, but in serenity. The future is basically a mystery, because today is basically a mystery as well. Today, as well as the future, admits of many problems. To confuse the two or place the wrong priorities on them, is to condemn both the present and the future.

Many skilled and beautiful books have been written on this topic of problem and mystery. A problem is not a mystery; life not only is a mystery itself, but abounds in mysteries. The fact is we often confuse the two and in this confusion we render the spiritual growth, which is our ardent desire, to a problem that seemingly will be solved by this or that adjustment; by this or that tactic; by this or that replacement of structure. The true believer in the victory of Christ must always profess in word and lifestyle that tomorrow's ills will not be solved by any simple exchange of this or that. The gift of the believer to his contemporaries is to powerfully and adequately express in his lifestyle that the problem is not with this or that thing, but rather with a whole mysterious underlying mode of life which draws its power and its strength from the fact of its union with the Lord Jesus. Too often what is proposed as an alternative to the suffering of today is unconnected with the basic center of energy from which alone the power to truly make a difference comes: the spirit. Too seldom is it ever heard at any discussion of the future that the basic ill and need for tomorrow is the uplifting humanizing presence of the Spirit of God. The spirit that makes possible the recognition of and living within the context of mystery. All too often what one hears is we will make more space available, have different kinds of education, melt down our firearms, not be concerned so much with monetary profit. Yet space does not in any way guarantee genuine dwelling. Life can flourish in a crowd and death can dwell in open spaces. Different kinds of education promise nothing but the possibility of a different kind of knowledge. To simply move from one to another guarantees the improvement of nothing. A person or nation can melt down its firearms and still not learn to live together. In fact, a person can melt down his guns and use the material to build a fence, which neither lets anyone in nor himself to escape. In the same way, lack of concern for monetary profit says only that I may be poor. It in no way says that this will give birth to not making material objects my top priority, let alone that it will allow me to approach all material things, be they the land, the water or the air, or bodies, in such a way that will allow them to reveal their inner nature to me. Poverty of itself is a most unworthwhile goal.

To suggest any one proposal for the future without taking into consideration that basically tomorrow is concerned with human life which is a mystery, runs the immense danger of replacing one bad element with an equally dead one. Nothing has been proved.

We will have new liturgy. We will have new structures. We will have new ways of celebrating our faith. We will march, we will picket, we will protest, we will have new schools, we will have better housing, we will demand our rights, and on and on the demand goes. By all means. But what is the heart of all these demands? Out of what wisdom do these demands spring? Where is their center of energy, to what are they directed? Are they merely solutions to problems that we seek, or have we perhaps finally arrived at a deeper, more productive level where we recognize mystery as mystery and treat it as such?

Morality of the Future

The future is very much a moral question. It is moral for it deals with the spirit. It is spiritual because it deals with human life. To make a man or nation aware of morality is to say that you have made him aware of the spiritual quality of human life. It is to introduce him to human suffering and joy, human failure and success. Morality presupposes that a man has a capacity to see what is happening around him. That he has the awareness of the values in his culture that either diminish or promote life. It presupposes that he has taken his adult responsibility to question, to seek, and to find. Involved in morality are the goals that a man holds as important, the values which constitute the very fabric of those goals, and the life that encompasses both. Only a living man can be a moral man, for only he makes decisions in favor of life or death, in favor of spirit or spirit denied.

The basic question for a believer facing the future is: Will I risk failure to achieve success? This is a moral question. For there is no risk if there is no weighing of values. There is no failure if there is no thought of attempting something better. There is no success if there is no awareness of the possibility of the pain of defeat. I cannot be moral if there is no awareness of the need for spiritual growth or the presence of repressed spirit. If I see no death, there can be no call to life. But if a man sees no death, how does he know the meaning of life?

The morality of the future arises out of the situation of seeing the need for life and deciding the role that we must play in its birth. It is a matter of uniting ourselves with the power of Christ crucified and risen, so that we may make the ultimate victory of Christ, rose-like, apparent in this world. It is to be concerned first of all with the real things which are the mysterious elements of human life. Elements such as pride, and dignity and human freedom.

But this is not easy. How great the temptation to reduce mysteries to problems and only then set hand to this phantom, non-existent plow. Great the temptation to fall before the challenge by claiming bitterness as the only realistic response to a world we choose to call dead, unmindful of all the many evidences of the great spiritual birth going on around us. At times indeed, we are tempted to join with the ancient skeptics who responded to unredeemed suffering by simply saying, "It has always been so; do not take it seriously."

The question of morality is the essential question of each one's personal response. For each response is basically either in favor of renewed life or against it. And on this altar, and this altar alone, is the bread of daily morality consecrated. Morality precisely asks if we take human life seriously. It asks if someone other than ourselves suffering or in need truly matters. The moral question is the fundamental question that Christ raises in our lives, challenging us to truly come alive to the spirit. It is the fundamental question of the future: Just how moral will man be? How moral does he see that he must be?

Conscience is the concrete expression of morality here and now. The entire question of the city of tomorrow rests upon the foundation of the conscience of the builders. For the only goal to which conscience strives is that of truth as it is seen. Men in search of truth, men not afraid of truth, are the only ones with whom the future has a chance. Truth not about this or that question of theory so much, but truth as it is lived. The truth of human suffering and human resurrection. The truth of the need to transcend the desire for material profit in favor of the urgent demand and splendor of human progress. Conscience is the sight that man uses in his quest for truth. If the eye is dark, how shall he find the light?

And if he finds not truth, what blueprint shall he use in the creation of the future?

Believers must hold that truth is power and it is power that alone can change the shape of the earth. A man who believes that an essential part of life is starvation, misery and wretchedness, will not lift a finger to change his situation or that of his suffering brothers. Yet, let the truth be revealed by his understanding of the meaning of life as sacred, and the strongest chains will not restrain him from raising his voice. Let him understand the meaning of life is spirit and freedom; let him know that life must mean the sharing of the good things of this earth; that education is not the sole privilege of the rich, and a new living believer will be born to share in the light.

But what is morality if it is not truth being unveiled; and what is conscience if it is not the present degree of truth available to all; and what is the substance of hope for the future if it is not the progressive realization of this truth for all; and what, indeed, is the risen Christ if it is not the ardent desire to bring all the goods of the earth to all our brothers?

Truth is the mightiest agent of transformation known to man. Transformation is the essence of Christianity. St. Paul continually calls out to the people for "Metanoia," or a progressive change of heart. Saint John the Baptist calls out to the people to re-form their lives. Christ was always heard to be saying that the Kingdom of God is at hand, renew yourselves and take hold of it. It is the truth of one's own self that projected into the future will be the form of that which we call Future. The truth of one's own redeemed self that affirms the need for the spirit in all of human life; the truth that cries out in the face of unnecessary avoidable suffering; the truth that one devours himself if in isolation he shares not his joys, dreams or pains.

When we are degraded, abused or used, every individual knows in himself that the whole world has been degraded by his misfortune. We believe that any man not able to provide sufficient material for his family's subsistence, will believe he deprived them of the bread of spiritual values and thus become an outcast among men. We know the hunger in our own hearts, for we ourselves have searched so ardently for it, for something or someone honest, for that which is a reality and not a spoken theory, for integrity that willingly endures suffering for the sake of truth. Within everyone is the heart knowledge more or less active, that given the opportunity, man would rather do good than evil; he would rather celebrate joy than inflict pain.

The question is: Will the truth which we all acknowledge in ourselves be allowed to form the breath of tomorrow? Will we be moral enough to let that truth live? Is our willingness to suffer, and the conviction of the need to transcend personal comfort sufficient to let the truth of ourselves fire the kiln from which tomorrow's bricks will be stamped?

It is moral to say yes to the mystery of life. It is immoral not to say no to that which stifles the birth of the spirit. There is much in our culture and every culture which allows life to prosper. There is much in our culture and every culture that says no to life. The moral stance for a believer, for it is of the spirit, is to see that culture is less than life. It is exceedingly difficult for one who has received only benefits and never been injured or deprived by his respective culture to understand how anyone else cannot share a full-hearted approval for the system in which he lives. Apparent prophets proclaim that any saying of no to that culture is being a traitor to the parent that provided him with such abundance. Yet, this fallacy is built upon the premise that culture and life are synonymous and that everyone has equally benefited from the goods that a culture has to offer.

Everyone does not share in the goods of any particular culture. If a man's conscience projects him on the search for truth, this soon becomes apparent. To say no to a man or group of people reaching out for the same privileges another person or group of people in that culture has enjoyed so long that they consider it a matter of course, is to say no to life. Not to care is to reject truth as it manifests itself. To say no to truth is the pinnacle of the immoral man.

But there is no such thing as any culture that delivers only good. The question is not one of merely refusing to see the true condition of ourselves. To see it and resist whatever in it promotes death. And a culture that directly or indirectly fosters a condition where its inhabitants are unaware of the suffering and deprivation of other people in their culture has great need of moral men to enlighten this area of darkness. Any culture that would equate itself with human dignity, considering all those not of that culture as basically inferior, is blind at its core. A culture that arrogantly equates power with force and attempts to inflict that pseudo-power upon others, is lame. And any of that culture who refuse to see the death are the true traitors, for they refuse to destroy that which makes a thing of beauty less than it could be. They are like gardeners who refuse to pluck the weeds from their gardens, even though eventually the weeds will kill all the flowers.

It is no more of truth to promote life than it is to resist death. There are many who would say yes to the good, but will not say no to the evil. They allow the weeds to defile their gardens. They stone those who would rip the weeds from the ground.

Morality is the search for truth. Truth is both the response yes and no. This response is made within the context of our own culture, for that is where we live. The moral man in the late 20th century has become aware that morality applies to the real things of life. He is conscious of the underlying direction of life in process in all those forces which give direction to that life. He is concerned above all else with truth, for in the light of truth alone can he see what needs to be affirmed and what denied.

The man of truth is the hope of the future, for only he can rise above his culture to embrace life as it is, life as it is lived in the hearts of all men in every country, including his own. Life and the meaning of life, as revealed to us by the Lord Jesus. Life abounding in hope and the promise of community, for we are one in the Father, as Christ in God and God in us.

2. ELECTION

In everyone's life there have been most important moments. Moments when decisions were made, sometimes in absolute certainty, sometimes plagued by half-doubt, and yet, they would affect the complexion of that life for as long as it lasted. Always these decisions were not generalizations, not theoretical abstractions. They centered around a specific tangible decision that a person, race, or even a world would have to make concerning itself. A decision such as when a country's leaders "go to war." The decision does not concern itself with the theory of war, but with the life and death of countless individuals. A decision in favor of peace does not concern itself with the condition of absence of war or the theoretical aspect of peace, but rather with the laying down of arms, the pounding of spears into plowshares. It concerns itself with those attitudes of mind and heart whereby brothers can live in harmony and reconciliation.

A person's decision to marry is concerned with: "Should I at this time marry this person?" It does not concern itself with the theory of love, but the realistic concrete decision about me, here and now. These moments dealing with family, business, God or whatever, are the finger-like influences reaching out to touch every part and parcel of our life. They take our lives like potter's clay and form us into whatever shape we shall be. The decision, as terrifying as it may be, concerns itself with whether or not we reach out for what seems to be something better than we have known. Man's ultimate tragedy is when seeing an avenue brightly lit, he chooses rather to travel a dim alley. His tragedy is seeing a treasure beyond a steep hill—he falters before the obstacles and never undertakes the climb. As the poet said, "Yonder hill testeth a man's heart, long before it testeth his legs."

Just so it is with accepting Christ's call to election. It is one thing to say yes, there is a Jesus, there is a pilgrimage. It is quite another thing to say there is Christ for me and the journey is mine. To know God is an opening door beckoning man to enter speaks of a possibility; to know that He is beckoning us, speaks of the actualization of the potential. The immense journey that man's mind and spirit has taken leading him to the rim of a magnificent lake only makes possible the decision to drink of the spirit or not, to pitch his tent by the richness of the clear water, it does not accomplish it. We, as every people in every age of every century, have the decision whether we will be of the Lord or not. Our question of faith is a terrifying yet necessary leap into the darkness to allow ourselves to be possessed of the Lord, to cling to the knowledge that Christ has won the victory through every storm. To allow the clarion call of Christ's word of election to breach the walls of our indifference, obtuseness and fear. To allow ourselves to dare to dream that the Kingdom is a possibility, that men can rise above themselves, and all fruits heavily hanging on the branches of that decision can be ours. It is our choice to make real the ardent plea of Pope Paul, "War never again."

To make a reality the visions of all dreamers and lovers of mankind as they prompt and urge us to make our own those qualities of heart whereby peace can come upon the earth. Election is an invitation that we are free to accept or reject.

John had just finished speaking to 70 senior high school boys. The subject was alcoholism. Even though the sounds of applause were still washing over him like a warm wave, he was possessed by a ponderous sadness. How its teeth sunk into him. John himself was an alcoholic. For longer than he cared to remember, his address had been the county jail. His list of arrests numbering close to one hundred, ranging all the way from assault to drunken driving. His sickness had caused him to lose his wife, children and his own sanity. He knew what it was all about from the inside out. Its smell, its taste, its feeling of immense failure. Then the most astounding of all human phenomena had befallen him, a spiritual awakening.

All of a sudden it wasn't good enough, this life of waste, and more importantly, he became aware that it didn't have to be. He was simply sick and tired of being sick and tired. John had hit bottom. That dawning had been 12 years ago. Since then, he has not only been sober, but his life has profoundly changed. Now there were many great joys in his life. The joy of seeing a bird fly, the sound of music, the sight of snow falling upon the ground. But the greatest of all his joys was the chance to speak to young people about where he had been, in the hope it might aid them in choosing a different direction. If only he could help one person avoid that long miserable road.

A boy walked the halls behind John. A skinny kid with long blond hair. He had just broken John's heart. The boy was like John's own shadow walking behind him. From the questions the lad had asked, John was sure that he had the disease of alcoholism. He was also sure that the boy was not conscious of it and had no intention of helping himself. He had not yet hurt enough.

Just as no human words could capture the joy, the immense power and light of his own spiritual awakening, so there were no words to describe the pain in looking at this walking reflection of himself of 20 years ago. The boy's life would be so very painful. Maybe he would never have a chance to come back. John had held out an invitation to something better; the boy had laughed. All John could do was sigh and walk out into the street. You can't push the river.

At one point in his life, Jesus too must have been similarly sad. There was a young man, perhaps not unlike the tall, thin blond whom John encountered. This young man in Jesus' life was wealthy. Jesus looked deep into the man's inner temple and must have seen much good. So much potential, if only he could free his heart for something better. With all possible kindness and truth, Jesus offered him a greater share in the building of a kingdom. All the young man had to do was take one standard of wealth in exchange for another. He had to face himself that he might be free, but he could not. The young man walked away; election had been rejected.

Matthew had accepted the same call. On just an ordinary day he sat at his booth collecting taxes. Matthew was a publican, and in great disfavor with the populace. It was a well-known fact that tax collectors levied much higher sums than were directed by Rome and kept the difference. No love was ever lost on a publican. Such was his occupation on that most ordinary day that was like none other. For on that day Jesus walked by and looked in, deeply so. He saw that this man could be so much more, and he was ready for more. In the simplest of words, Scripture describes Jesus saying, "Follow Me." Luke reports, "Matthew left everything behind, rose and followed Him." The tax collector-turned-apostle was the subject of election. He had recognized the invitation for what it was and accepted it.

Christ encountered many people in His time. To them He offered an invitation to life that they might share it with others. He called them forth as children of election. Some accepted, some did not. The power that Christ was offering them was theirs to be taken. They, in their turn, could have recreated their present, and in doing so, reached out the promise of a brighter future for all who would come after them. There were many who had just bought a farm, or found it imperative to try out a new team of oxen. One even had more legitimate reluctance to follow this harbinger of a new sunrise. He begged, "Let me first bury my dead father." Jesus' response, at first, seems cruel and insensitive, "Let the dead bury their own dead." However, in the view of Christ's own sadness over the death of His friend, Lazarus, and His willingness to take care of all people in trouble, we understand that the meaning of this response was simply that the time of your call is now, put nothing as a greater priority.

We are the modern versions of these, our

brothers and sisters. We are the children of election today, called upon to make this day all it can be and, therefore, make the promise of the future as bright as possible. Life goes before us. Some accept the risk involved in the Carpenter's secret, and some do not. How easily a modern-day evangelist could re-write the chapters of election in the gospel of everyday life, ". . . and Jesus came upon a man in the midst of hungrily acquiring a new car and asked, 'How important is that new car to you?' He came upon a person busily making himself acceptable to polite society, anxious to be accepted at all costs. He came upon a man whose business took up all his time, whose pursuit of fun left no time for living. He came upon a man shooting pool, a woman playing bridge, all legitimate activities, and to each one He held up the prism of His message, so that their lives passing through it would divide into its separate parts revealing its own unique view and promise of completeness. To each one with gentle insistence, He asked, 'What are you doing? What are you becoming? I have a great work for you, follow Me.' With great joy the Son of God came upon a man in the prime of a full life. He asked the young man to follow Him, to work the exchange of what is for what could be. The man said, 'Not now, Lord, wait. Wait until I feel the need of you. Wait until I am old and have had my fun, and I will be your disciple then, your secret-bearer. But don't ask me now.' And Jesus turned sadly away.

"But to others He came. He came to a man who could brilliantly teach in the inner city, and the man said yes. He came to the man who could rise above his own particular calvary, and the man said yes. He came to so many who would dare face their demons and their obstacles, and so many replied yes, and have never ceased becoming what they could be."

It may be terrifying for people accustomed to reliance on science, the machine, pills, and the expertise of experts, to hear that the core of life, the very heart of the world, is in our hands. But for us who are the children of election today, it is still the case. We are the ones called forth in this day to be of royal priesthood, to raise up a holy people. We are life's momentary result of mankind's ancient impulse to develop minds that can see through the surface of things, minds capable of understanding there is much we can never understand. We are the beings whose spiritual capacity enables us to love or hate. We can kill wantonly or cause life to rise from the ashes. It has taken countless centuries and the combined spiritual energy of all people of all ages, plus the intervention of the Son of God into our consciousness, to bring us to this point. This point of understanding that the world now at this moment has been entrusted to our tending. It does little good to write endless poetry concerning the building up of the earth, or fashioning a better tomorrow from the raw materials of today, if we do not first cross the threshold of acknowledging that the decision to accomplish this task of the Lord is ours. It is we who must do it. The past is past; we are the Matthews, the Lukes and the Marys of today.

But They Were Holy

Somehow it seems acceptable, even easy, to believe that great men like Abraham, Moses or Paul, having receivied a clear-cut call from God, should hear and follow. After all, they were special people. They were holy. They understood their call and had the strength to accomplish it. It is different with us.

But was it so simple? As far as students of ancient history know, Abraham was the only man on the face of the earth at that time who believed in monotheism, the worship of one Supreme God. He lived in the midst of pagans, men who worshipped many gods. How radically different he must have been from his contemporaries. Exactly how the spiritual awakening occurred in Abraham's life, no one knows. But somehow from the practice of paganism which he embraced, he experienced God inflaming him with an unheard of truth: there is one God. I am He. Come apart and worship Me. You will be my seed-bearer, fathering a great nation, who one day after a great journey, will know Me with all of your hearts.

Abraham's wife must have thought he was insane. Here he was, a man well into his years, believed to be quite well-to-do, an established goatherder, and the father of a large clan. Yet here he was suggesting to leave it all; to take their possessions, their clan, and to go off on a long pilgrimage into an unknown land, and why? Why do such an outlandish, imprudent thing? All poor Abraham could do, as millions after him, was explain that it was just inside him. He knew that this was what must be done.

Even more so later, realizing that he was to be the father of a great nation, and having no children, he was asked to sacrifice to the Lord, his only son

Isaac. How indeed could he follow such a call? Was this not clearly a contradiction? How could he sacrifice his only son, and yet be the father of a great nation who would be more numerous than the grains of sand on a seashore? Perhaps it wasn't quite as easy for Abraham as we might think.

Moses' call came six hundred years later, and was no less radical. How was he, an unknown shepherd, possibly to demand from the ruler of the mightiest nation on earth the release of his enslaved people? Not beg or ask, but demand. If this were not enough, his call to election instructed him to threaten extreme punishment if his demands were not met. All of this not in behalf of some enslaved, but powerful people. Rather, he was beseeching in behalf of a patchwork, loose association of desert tribes. The wondrous signs to be performed by Moses were not offered by a mighty enemy king, but rather by the supposed God of these enslaved people. How could anyone take seriously the God of people who were slaves?

The sacrament of Moses' call of election resulted from a mysterious encounter with the burning bush. A burning bush that somehow symbolized the burning spirit of this man Moses and the presence of God who would be with him always. Whatever the exact meaning of the symbolism of the bush, a door opened in this desert shepherd. There was a call and a response. Not an easy call, nor an easy response.

Biblical scholars eloquently trace the passing of the torch of God-consciousness from one age to another, from one century to another. With each succeeding era, the burning bush gathered strength and light to itself, as men of election, at times regal

kings, at others peasant farmers, accepted their call
and pushed back, if only fractionally, the darkness of
human consciousness concerning the God of light.
The torch was carried out of Egypt, yet nearly sput-
tered out in the desert before a golden calf. It
flourished in the age of conquest, when the Walls of
Jericho fell, and the lost tribes became a nation.
Through two disastrous military defeats, and as
many exiles into slavery, the torch burned. Increas-
ing in wisdom and depth through the instrument of
God's people of election, prophets came and went.
Kings wrapped royal purple around themselves,
while their spirits became evermore threadbare.
With the unstoppable momentum of time itself, the
God-consciousness grew, the torch passing across the
face of the earth carried by the men of election. God
simply was not satisfied with no one knowing there
was but one God. Nor was He content to have men
deaf, dumb and blind to His plan for man. Man
must know His way for human growth and happiness. They must know that He, God, was their Father, and they in their turn were brothers to one
another, united in the breaking of the bread. They
must claim their spiritual energy to recreate the face
of the earth.

And so the torch began its journey. Through
Abraham, Moses, Solomon and David. Through the
prophets and judges. Through a man named John,
whom we call the Baptist, and the mother of a carpenter, named Mary. Jesus, himself, of course, was
the supreme recipient of election. He was the ultimate fulfiller of the dream of God for Man. As
foggy and smoky as the torch had been through all
the ages of pilgrimage, Jesus would eliminate the

mist and blow away the smoke, making crystal-clear
who this God was whom He defined as Father, and
John paints for us as Love. In His teachings, message, and the indisputable testimony of His life, we
would be able to grasp what is required of us by our
Father. And again from this new vantage point of
Christ, in whom all things are new, the torch began
its journey to our decade, to our very doorstep.

Through the persecution of Nero, the royal af-
firmation of Constantine in the year 333, the great
ages of missionary zeal and into the gloom of those
centuries we call the Dark Ages, the torch is passed.
At times faltering, apparently near extinction; at
others, seemingly blazing in glorious light. But
always carried forth by the men of election, whose
job it was to make the sharing in the light of God
through Christ for all people more attainable and
available.

Such seemingly isolated and minorly important
events as the invention of the printing press, gun-
powder, steam, and the development of our contemporary understanding of money, profoundly influenced the lives of whole continents. Complete
ways of living passed away. Famine, disease and
general unrest drove countless others to seek the op-
portunities offered by this new country, America.
The age of immigration was on. With the human
tide rolling in, came men of election among them.
Modern-day prophets, who like their ancestors, went
into a strange land with their countrymen, not to
prosper or carve out an empire, but to keep the torch
brightly lit. Wars, depressions, economic booms and
busts, all the problems that go both with affluence

and poverty, abound. And to all of this incomprehensible flow of history, the secret of Jesus must speak. But whose mouth will be used? Whose spirit will cradle the meaning of the words spoken? Whose heart will carry them into actuality, if not those who had the ability to hear? And in hearing, had responded, and in responding to their personal call, have accepted the torch handed them from centuries back and carried forward by their spiritual ancestors? Ancestors, who clearly saw their work was the work of the Lord. Whose work is the redemption and humanizing of all people, His people, to witness by their lives that it is possible to celebrate in joy the adventure of living; to confront the human condition around them, and leave it better than they found it.

How thrilling, unutterably thrilling, to trace all the lines of ancestry from our own doors back into the dim caverns of long ago.

This year, this day, this hour, we are the recipients of the physical gift of our bodies from creatures who danced long ago around the fire of a pre-Ice Age year, slowly groping for the hard-won doors, whose entrance would allow us to think, to reason, to love if we so chose; we are the spiritual benefactors of prophets who were stoned and laughed at and scorned; slaves who rushed out of Egypt under the command of a strange, stuttering man named Moses. The circuitry of our minds bears the lasting imprint of emperors and kings, saints and philosophers, whose decisions and struggles pushed back the frontiers of non-understanding until the brightness of wisdom so freely given us lies about us as stones of flint awaiting someone to liberate the magical fire within. We are the recipients of the unthinkable knowledge given us by the Lord, that death has been confronted and bested.

Within us are all these men and the Son of God Himself, present in our ability to think, feel, care, love—our potential to open to the mystery of faith. They wait, observant, hopeful, as spectators at some monumental event, who have given their lives to bring the contest thus far, awaiting our decision, our willingness to carry the torch an inch further. The light of lights has passed from them to us. It is our struggle, our time, and our decision. Let no one think himself unimportant or impotent in the creation of the world. Let no one dare, in the face of such important matters as bringing life to others and to this earth, fail by giving into despair or depression, for the Lord has won, and He calls us to share in this victory.

3. SPIRIT

How? How indeed shall this marvelous transformation of the face of the earth take place? Obviously, it is beyond the power of man to transform man, and even within the bravest dreamer of dreams, the vision of what can be fades without a realistic belief in the ability to accomplish the vision. But how? From whence the power?

In response to such valid doubts and questions in the time of Our Lord, Christ promised that His first gift to those who believe would be His spirit. The spirit of Christ is the very heart and soul, the very foundation of the Kingdom of God.

All great men, when they die, bequeath their spirits to their life's work. But it is never quite the same once a man's physical presence is gone. No matter how vital his spirit might have been, how profound his influence, when a man dies he is of the past. His contribution lives on at the mercy of other men to bend, twist, and water down what he has built up. Jesus, in many important ways, is the exception.

In willing His spirit to the community of man, to His secret-bearers, Jesus gave us not only the inspiring force that influenced all He did and said, but a resident person of God upon the earth. Christ's spirit is as much tied to this earth because of God's love, as is the sun and the rolling hills. Present as a person, not a memory. A spirit that could not diminish or run out of energy. A spirit that would be as alive and active in our own times as in ages past.

Spirit by its very nature is intangible, yet nothing is more concrete. The presence of the spirit was the difference between the Apostles' befuddlement on Friday, and the burning zeal on the day called Pentecost. The flat denial, "I do not know the man," was concrete enough, yet so were the nails driven into the hands of Peter on his upside-down throne. The difference in the two scenes: Jesus' first gift to those who believe, His spirit. His spirit, alone, which initiates and makes permanent the experience which leads to conversion.

The forms of this experience may differ. The effects of the spirit's presence, however, are always the same. Apathy, doubt, meaningless, give way to rebirth; servitude to the dry letter of the law yields to liberation; from viewing God's covenant as burden, the spirit calls up the certitude of our vocation of election. Shameful debilitating priorities of life melt under the breath of God, remolding us into the servants of God, as Jesus himself was. The Pentecost liturgy begs the spirit to "wash our sinful stains away, water from heaven our barren clay, our wounds and bruises heal, to your sweet yoke our stiff necks bow, warm with your love our hearts of snow, our wandering feet recall."

"Warm our hearts of snow . . ." From how many throats does the world cry out for a warming of cold hearts? How many hearts are terrified to walk the streets, afraid to go to bed for fear of what awaits them in their own inner darkness? How many of our brothers and sisters are debased and humiliated, in ways that lead to divorce courts, prisons and mental wards? How much need is there for the seven-fold gifts to invade this ghost-ridden world? There are demons that plague us in the guise of guilt, frustration and alienation. There are truly evil spirits that coax many a heart to give up, to hope for nothing because there is nothing more than the endless round of work, back home to their television and spirit-empty meals, then to bed, then back to work.

But it doesn't have to be. With the presence of the spirit of God residing in our hearts and our minds, there is a real and realistic possibility of the peace of Christ to be with us. The peace of Christ is the gift of Shalom to those who believe.

Shalom, Peace Be With You. Shalom, said the patch sewed to the leg of the long-haired girl's jeans. Shalom read the sign in the Jewish restaurant. Shalom said the stationery used by the nuns. Shalom, Peace, good wishes, Shalom—I wish you clean air to breathe. Shalom my friend, may your business venture prosper. Shalom, traveler, may your roads lead you home. Shalom, old man, may your sons bring you pleasure. Shalom, young man, may the world be like clay and you the potter's hands. Shalom, young girl, may wisdom and innocence be to you like the two halves of a circle making one.

Shalom seems to be the gift worded in many different ways people of this age wish one another. Shalom is the Peace of Christ. It is the gift given us by Christ from the Father, to be our gift to one another. But Shalom is the enfleshment of the spirit reaching from one's temple to another. If there is no spirit, no seeing of life as art, no ability to sing a tough song, no saying of both yes and no, all of which are apples hanging on the same tree of the spirit, then there can be no Shalom.

Shalom is so many things, so many abilities. The ability to die for the sake of rising, to give and to receive, to love and to reject, to be and yet to see the option of diminishing. To love self enough to understand that the greatest love is to allow others to prosper. Perhaps right here is the key: understanding. Shalom is to understand first of all what it means to understand. To know that my heart needs a fellow traveler walking the same roads, fighting the same battles, soaking his feet in the same streams. Shalom is to grasp that understanding is more than intelligence, and to be open to the conscious communication of my fellow man in ways deeper than words. Shalom is to understand that I am only half a circle, seeking its other half to join in strength, to make its long journey, someone with whom I have an understanding. If there is someone with whom I can share a secret in this whole world, then its ugliness is not so desperate, and its beauty increased tenfold. Not just someone else who, with me, is joyful or miserable, but another human being who understands what I am saying.

Shalom, or peace, is a growing kind of thing. It creeps up on a person like the rising sun creeps up on the world. But the tones of peace and dawning spirit in a person's life are much richer than the most beautiful colors that stream from the burning sun. They are just not as obvious to the unpracticed eye. You must know what you are looking for to see spirit-in-man grow, but it is everywhere. Your eye must be clear enough for the spirit to penetrate. It's all so subtle, as with Julie.

If ever there was a most beautiful little princess, it was Julie. There she was for the first time in her life, at a fancy dinner theater. Her peasant dress reached all the way to the floor, almost five feet down. A little medal hung around her neck that said, "Peace" and was shaped like a dove, but there was no peace. The place scared her. Even though she was nineteen, she was totally alien to what was going on. If it were a drive-in movie, a bar, a street corner, then that would be okay, she knew all about these. She knew all about rock music and what it meant to be used. In fact, she knew so much about this that she took it for granted there could be nothing else.

Julie's personality is like a skyrocket: flashy, colorful, powerful. That is, until anyone begins to walk dangerously close to her core. As soon as someone, anyone, says anything honest to her or invites her to really say who she is, there is an abrupt dead-end. Her motto simply stated is: I'm tough; I need no one.

This particular dinner theater is a buffet style. Each customer was expected to walk through the line to get his dinner. Even though Julie was more beautiful than anyone there, she didn't want to be there, and was terrified to walk through the line. What if she did something wrong? What if she said the wrong thing? What if these people saw her and laughed at her? She would ten times rather fake being sick, eat nothing, than walk through the line. If only the carpet was a little deeper, she would love to sink into it and disappear. How desperately she needed a healing community.

The people with her would have no part of that. What good is it to be special if you don't know it?

Finally, she made it through the buffet aisle shaking
like a leaf. Thank God when the lights went out and
the play started. Darkness is a good hiding place.
But how wide the eyes of the spirit were looking out.

The play was about a crazy man who had a
quest in life to see the good, to celebrate virtue, to
dream the impossible dream. There was a girl in the
play as well. Her spirit was much like Julie's. She
thought she was trash; she trusted no one. She wanted nothing, and she expected nothing. There was absolutely no spirit in her life and, therefore, there was
no peace and no Shalom. The crazy man didn't see
things that way. He gave her a new name, as Christ
often did when His spirit touched someone. He told
her that she was a great lady. His actions and lifestyle toward her offered a new vision of what could
be, and who knows, even, maybe, what should be. He
convinced her that she was special, indeed, a wonderful, beautiful woman.

The lights came back on in more ways than just
the theater. Walking out, Julie didn't want to touch
anyone. She didn't want to get very close. She didn't
even say much. You must know what you are looking for to see Shalom. The question was there. The
deep dark question in her spirit. Was she, could she,
be like the woman in the play? Something more than
the terrible thing that she thinks she is? The possibility of the opening rose had bloomed. Lazarus had
come back from the tomb. For she was there, which
meant someone cared enough to convince her to go.
Who knows, maybe her friends were as crazy as the
man in the play.

The little peace medal looked the same before
the play as after, but the woman wasn't. As Julie

grows, if she does, and the knowledge that she is as special as she truly is, she could tell you all about Shalom. Tell you, because it would be happening to her.

The presence of Christ's spirit, which is the source of all authentic human life and our only promise for the future, is desperately needed in our society today. But this presence is made possible only by the coming of the spirit into our hearts. The spirit that seals into our very being the certitude that we are the children of election, the builders of the kingdom, the light on the mountain that dispels the darkness. None but the spirit of God is the measure and liberator of our power. Again, not power in the sense of violent force of bullets and guns, of bending someone else to our will. But power in the sense of liberating someone else to be all that he can be. It is the creative potential that roams about, often un-born in the inner corridors of our being. We have that potential. It is born to each one of us. Every man can be uncommon in the way of the spirit of God. Is there anyone who could not bring a slave of fear to life with his friendship, anyone who could not liberate one bound and indentured to loneliness to the sun of the happy life, by extending that knowl-edge that they are loved? Is there anyone who could not go an extra mile with someone trudging past our doors and thereby give him the strength to finish his appointed task? And if this is not power, then Jesus had no gift to give, nor we to our brothers.

The ancient judges of Israel were called by the spirit and touched by spiritual experiences. Without expecting it, with nothing to pre-dispose them, they were snatched from ordinary life, and called to a mighty work. Samson, Gideon and Saul were suddenly and totally changed. Not just made capable of doing exceptional deeds, but invested with new qualities of their personalities, which allowed them to act as liberators of their people. Their genius, their power was freed, thus making them able in an extraordinary manner to carry out the mission of God.

So within us, the spirit would summon forth greatness. He would call us to become such a people as would not tolerate the intolerable. People who not only could, but would, care beyond all else for the human, lovely world God has given us to care for. The spirit would actualize that genius.

"I have little to offer; what can I do?" is a typical response, but blind. All of life is a meeting. The great Jewish scholar Martin Buber paints for us the vision of life as dialogue. Dialogue in that everything of meaning in our world exists within the space of a relationship, within that space passing between an I and a Thou. Each one of us has an opportunity to express our awareness of the election that is ours within that space of relationship. Each one an invitation to dispose another for the spiritual awakening of being thought worthy enough to at least be noticed, and thereby growing ourselves. Each meeting, if we could see it, is a chance to give hope, to assure the other that life must not merely be endured, but is realistically able to be celebrated and lived. The spirit both frees us to receive and to give, to heal and be healed.

The spirit is Shalom, and Shalom is to undertake the process of resurrection. It is not for man to say the nature of the resurrection outside of the context of time or beyond the door of death. What is for man to say is about the resurrection that must go on every day, the resurrection that is now. It is not a resurrection after life, but during life. It is not a giving up or a freeing from the body, but a resurrection in the body. It is not a rescuing out of life, but a submerging into it. All of which sounds very, very foolish to a great many people.

To many brothers and sisters life is duty, and duty is drudgery, and drudgery is being responsible. And being responsible is what I must do and there is no room for resurrection. For others the whole notion of people rising above their limitations is mere fallacy.

But there is room for resurrection wherever there is room for spirit. Spirit infallibly calls forth resurrection and "coming forth" is the purpose of life. There is the possibility of people to see the world with their souls and not just with their eyes. To see all the Joyces and Julies and say, "Come. Come live within my love." To more than hear sounds, but to understand what they mean. It is possible to say we are "just men," and mean being able to do great things. One can say there is honesty, ruthless gut-level honesty, not as a theory, but as a lived reality. It is possible to say there is love, which puts others' good above my own simple wants, which says "I love you," and does not mean I am going to destructively use you. There is such a thing as Shalom and serenity and peace of life that is not achieved by saying there is no evil, but by not losing my ability to celebrate life, even while I resist death. Love, honesty, serenity are resurrection, for they are spirit manifesting itself in people's lives. But I can only believe that if someone shows me by his life that it is possible. This is the only Word that is credible. From this pinpoint of electrifying consciousness comes the challenge and the thrill of our call of election. From this exact point comes our responsibility of living the future and projecting all that is best of the spirit in ourselves into tomorrow.

A man can for years or hours talk of the resurrection, what it means, how it was thought of through the centuries, what other theologians think it will be. Fine. But this does not cause the resurrection to happen. Ultimately, it must happen within ourselves. Resurrection, if it is to be real, must be our own experience. It occurs in our dawning. In our own experience of life. If it doesn't happen there, then all you can do is talk about it as something outside of yourself.

But resurrection is an inside thing. Every man is a theologian, for he is the temple, and his heart is the altar, and his life is the bread, and his love is the breaking of that bread. Into every man's life the urgent quest of spirit to be born comes. The spirit that is light seeking resurrection.

As is obvious today, buttons are in. They say everything. Some funny, some not so funny. One looked funny at first, then it said something quite different. The face on the button said, "Is there a chance of life after birth?" Is there?

But we are alive, aren't we? We're here able to read the button, to laugh about it, to buy it. If you're already alive, who can question it? But are we? Resurrection kind of alive? Zest for living alive? Serenity alive? Spirit alive? For Julie there is a dawning, a coming from the grave, for someone has rolled the stone away. Or at least offered her the chance of

stepping forth in the newness of life. Into her consciousness came the truth. That it is possible to form
a relationship not based upon destructively using
someone. That it was possible someone could authentically and truly care about her beyond his own
selfish wants and conveniences. But for every Julie
there are so many more. So many more who are
trapped in office buildings, in loveless homes, on the
street corner, and on huge campuses. So many who
need someone to do battle for them. To prove that it
is a fact that life need not be just a dog-fight. That
people can relate to one another in a way that
creates and frees. Whatever resurrection awaits these
prisoners of this world after life, fine, but right now
the need is different. Right now they need to see, to
touch and to feel resurrection of the living, not the
dead. The need to know that there is life now, not
just after the grave.

How in truth can the kingdom come, the world
come to completion? How will the resurrection of
the earth take place within the context of the living?
By what unheard-of magic will people attempt the
task of listening, of giving to another the feast of a
good life? What in the name of God justifies the
bigger-than-imaginable expectation, no matter what
the cross a person must carry, that realistically proclaims truths as Shalom and serenity are possible?
And to what possible destiny do we, as a race, journey?

The answer, if the mystery of life and even the
greater mystery of God can be called an "answer,"
was first given to us by Jesus long ago. It is not a
scientific, mechanical answer, but an insight. It is
not a destination, but the direction of a journey to be

taken. It was the gift of the spirit. The spirit which alone liberates the genius of man to become man, which is to liberate his own capacity to be human, so that he, with his God, can renew the face of the earth. To this glorious undertaking we all are called. We are all to be roses lifting our heads to the sun and casting the sweetness of our spirits upon the wind.